大学英语立体化网络化系列教材　　　　　　　总主编　李淑静

②

博雅英语

BOYA College English

主　编：蒋学清
副主编：丁　研　李京平
编　者：（按姓氏拼音排列）
　　　　　　　　丁　研　郝运慧
　　　　　　　　　　　　敦来

北京大学出版社
PEKING UNIVERSITY PRESS

图书在版编目(CIP)数据

博雅英语.2 / 蒋学清主编. —北京:北京大学出版社,2015.11
(大学英语立体化网络化系列教材)
ISBN 978-7-301-25417-2

Ⅰ.①博…　Ⅱ.①蒋…　Ⅲ.①英语—高等学校—教材　Ⅳ.①H31

中国版本图书馆CIP数据核字(2015)第018125号

书　　名	博雅英语(2) BOYA YINGYU
著作责任者	蒋学清　主编
责 任 编 辑	刘　爽
标 准 书 号	ISBN 978-7-301-25417-2
出 版 发 行	北京大学出版社
地　　址	北京市海淀区成府路205号　100871
网　　址	http://www.pup.cn　　新浪微博:@北京大学出版社
编辑部邮箱	pupwaiwen@pup.cn
总编室邮箱	zpup@pup.cn
电　　话	邮购部 62752015　发行部 62750672　编辑部 62754382
印 刷 者	三河市北燕印装有限公司
经 销 者	新华书店
	787毫米×1092毫米　16开本　11.25印张　450千字 2015年11月第1版　2023年8月第3次印刷
定　　价	48.00元(配有光盘)

未经许可,不得以任何方式复制或抄袭本书之部分或全部内容。
版权所有,侵权必究
举报电话:010-62752024　电子信箱:fd@pup.pku.edu.cn
图书如有印装质量问题,请与出版部联系,电话:010-62756370

《博雅英语》专家委员会
（按姓氏拼音排列）

程朝翔　丁宏为　郭文革　胡壮麟
蒋学清　李淑静　林毅夫　凌　斌
刘意青　吕随启　申　丹　谭　颖
王义遒　张文霞　周小仪

前　言

古希腊罗马倡导的博雅教育(Liberal Education)，旨在传授广博的知识，培养独立完善的人格和优雅的气质，使人不仅获得专业技能，而且陶冶品学才识，成为完全的人。与之相辉映，中华文化传统如《论语》之"子曰：君子不器"，以及《大学》之"大学之道，在明明德，在亲民，在止于至善"，也强调人应该有完善的人格，不能像器具一样，只满足某一种用途。

北京大学教材建设委员会设立的大学英语教材改革项目《博雅英语》，正是要达到这样的目的，将大学英语课程的工具性和人文性有机统一，使之作为高等学校人文教育的一部分，体现高等教育区别于基础教育的特点，以教材的思想性带动语言学习，不仅增强学生的英语综合应用能力和自主学习能力，而且发展学生的跨文化交际能力和批判性思维能力。

人文性目标首先体现在对教学材料的选择上。《博雅英语》通过走访人文社科领域学者和调研学习者需求，在选材上确定了"语言与文学、历史与文明、哲学与人生、建筑与艺术、法制与民主、经济与社会、人与自然、科技与教育"等八个主题板块。所选听读材料既有中西方经典作品或其介绍，也有对现实生活中普世热点问题的分析或讨论，力图达到经典与时代的结合、西方文化与中华文化的互动、人文素养与科学精神的交融，彰显教育的根本——立德树人，使学生在批判性的英语学习中，吸收优秀的文化、观念和正确的价值观，培养跨文化国际视野和中国情怀，树立文化自觉和文化自信，未来成为中外文化交流及"讲好中国故事、传播好中国声音、阐释好中国特色"的重要力量。

在教学材料的编排上，《博雅英语》遵循语言学习发展规律，力图贯彻"以输入为基础、以输出为驱动"的理念，注重经典阅读、培养思辨能力、强化书面及口头表达能力。每个主题单元都由四个板块构成：视听导入(Lead-in)、从读到写(Reading and Writing)、从读到说(Reading and Speaking)、跨文化交流(Cross Cultural Communication)，以听读促写、以听读促说、以英汉互译促跨文化学习及中国文化传播，融合听说读写译各种语言技能，促进学生综合语言应用能力的养成。在学习活动的设计中，《博雅英语》尤其注重开放性，启发学生对经典的感受能力，培养批判性思维习惯，引导学生主动学习、自主学习和个性化地学习，培养发现问题、分析问题、解决问题的创新能力。

《博雅英语》力求构建优质的教学资源共享体系，发挥好教材在引导教师转变教学观念、调整教学方式等方面的功能和作用。在提供学生用书、教师用书及相应的电子资源的同时，还将组织授课教师围绕教材的重点、难点、疑点或某些教学环节开发微课，以视频为主要载体记录并分享其教育教学活动的精彩，并通过开放性的网络平台鼓励师生共同构建教学资源，交流学习成果，营造出一个个真实的微教学资源环境和学习共同体。

在大学英语课程改革不断深化的新阶段，全体编者期望通过编写《博雅英语》，为丰富大学英语课程的人文内涵、实现其工具性与人文性的有机统一、促进学生的综合素质提高和全面发展尽自己内绵薄之力。不足之处难免，敬请批评指正。

李淑静
2015年5月

Content

UNIT 1　LANGUAGE AND LITERATURE ·································· 1

　　Part One　　　　Lead-in ·································· 2
　　　　　　　　　　Section 1　Listening　A Psalm of Life ·································· 2
　　　　　　　　　　Section 2　Watching ·································· 3
　　Part Two　　　　Reading and Writing ·································· 4
　　　　　　　　　　Text A　The Autobiography of Benjamin Franklin ·································· 4
　　Part Three　　　Reading and Speaking ·································· 12
　　　　　　　　　　Text B　Why Do We Read Fiction? ·································· 12
　　Part Four　　　 Cross Cultural Communication ·································· 17
　　　　　　　　　　Passage A　许渊冲翻译理论的中国特色 ·································· 17
　　　　　　　　　　Passage B　Tradition and the Individual Talent ·································· 19

UNIT 2　WAR AND CIVILIZATION ·································· 21

　　Part One　　　　Lead-in ·································· 22
　　　　　　　　　　Section 1　Listening ·································· 22
　　　　　　　　　　Section 2　Watching ·································· 22
　　Part Two　　　　Reading and Writing ·································· 23
　　　　　　　　　　Text A　Grant and Lee: A Study in Contrasts ·································· 23
　　Part Three　　　Reading and Speaking ·································· 32
　　　　　　　　　　Text B　Soviet Strong Man ·································· 32
　　Part Four　　　 Cross Cultural Communication ·································· 36
　　　　　　　　　　Passage A　黄埔军校简史 ·································· 36
　　　　　　　　　　Passage B　A Brief History of West Point ·································· 37

UNIT 3　THE ROAD TO HAPPINESS ·································· 40

　　Part One　　　　Lead-in ·································· 41
　　　　　　　　　　Section 1　Listening　The Things that Make Americans Happy ·································· 41
　　　　　　　　　　Section 2　Watching ·································· 42

	Part Two	Reading and Writing	44
		Text A On Happiness	44
	Part Three	Reading and Speaking	54
		Text B Hamburger Model of Happiness	54
	Part Four	Cross Cultural Communication	60
		Passage A 获得相对幸福和绝对幸福的方法	60
		Passage B Platonic Harmony	62

UNIT 4 ARCHITECTURE OF THE WORLD 65

	Part One	Lead-in	66
		Section 1 Listening	66
		Section 2 Watching	66
	Part Two	Reading and Writing	67
		Text A In Search of Ancient Chinese Architecture	67
	Part Three	Reading and Speaking	78
		Text B The Sydney Opera House	78
	Part Four	Cross Cultural Communication	86
		Passage A 中国建筑本土化	86
		Passage B Chicago School Architecture	87

UNIT 5 LAW AND SOCIETY 90

	Part One	Lead-in	91
		Section 1 Listening	91
		Section 2 Watching	91
	Part Two	Reading and Writing	92
		Text A Law and Society	92
	Part Three	Reading and Speaking	100
		Text B The Function of Law	100
	Part Four	Cross Cultural Communication	106
		Passage A 权力的兽性	106
		Passage B	107

UNIT 6 DEMAND, PRICE AND WEALTH 110

	Part One	Lead-in	111
		Section 1 Listening	111
		Section 2 Watching	111

	Part Two	Reading and Writing ⋯⋯⋯⋯⋯⋯⋯⋯⋯⋯⋯⋯⋯⋯⋯⋯⋯⋯⋯	112
		Text A Gradations of Consumers' Demand ⋯⋯⋯⋯⋯⋯⋯⋯	112
	Part Three	Reading and Speaking ⋯⋯⋯⋯⋯⋯⋯⋯⋯⋯⋯⋯⋯⋯⋯⋯⋯	121
		Text B Yes, the Wealthy Can Be Deserving ⋯⋯⋯⋯⋯⋯⋯⋯	121
	Part Four	Cross Cultural Communication ⋯⋯⋯⋯⋯⋯⋯⋯⋯⋯⋯⋯⋯⋯	127
		Passage A 泛论生产事业 ⋯⋯⋯⋯⋯⋯⋯⋯⋯⋯⋯⋯⋯⋯⋯⋯⋯	127
		Passage B Of the Origin and Use of Money ⋯⋯⋯⋯⋯⋯⋯⋯	128

UNIT 7   BETWEEN TWO WORLDS ⋯⋯⋯⋯⋯⋯⋯⋯⋯⋯⋯⋯⋯⋯⋯⋯⋯⋯⋯⋯ 131

	Part One	Lead-in ⋯⋯⋯⋯⋯⋯⋯⋯⋯⋯⋯⋯⋯⋯⋯⋯⋯⋯⋯⋯⋯⋯⋯⋯⋯	132
		Section 1 Listening ⋯⋯⋯⋯⋯⋯⋯⋯⋯⋯⋯⋯⋯⋯⋯⋯⋯⋯	132
		Section 2 Watching ⋯⋯⋯⋯⋯⋯⋯⋯⋯⋯⋯⋯⋯⋯⋯⋯⋯⋯	132
	Part Two	Reading and Writing ⋯⋯⋯⋯⋯⋯⋯⋯⋯⋯⋯⋯⋯⋯⋯⋯⋯⋯⋯	133
		Text A The World We Have Lost ⋯⋯⋯⋯⋯⋯⋯⋯⋯⋯⋯⋯	133
	Part Three	Reading and Speaking ⋯⋯⋯⋯⋯⋯⋯⋯⋯⋯⋯⋯⋯⋯⋯⋯⋯	142
		Text B Saving the Amazon: Winning the war on ⋯⋯⋯⋯⋯⋯ deforestation	142
	Part Four	Cross Cultural Communication ⋯⋯⋯⋯⋯⋯⋯⋯⋯⋯⋯⋯⋯⋯	148
		Passage A 大气污染防治行动计划 ⋯⋯⋯⋯⋯⋯⋯⋯⋯⋯⋯⋯	148
		Passage B London Air Quality ⋯⋯⋯⋯⋯⋯⋯⋯⋯⋯⋯⋯⋯ Strategy 2011—2015	149

UNIT 8   TECHNOLOGY AND MEDIA ⋯⋯⋯⋯⋯⋯⋯⋯⋯⋯⋯⋯⋯⋯⋯⋯⋯⋯⋯ 152

	Part One	Lead-in ⋯⋯⋯⋯⋯⋯⋯⋯⋯⋯⋯⋯⋯⋯⋯⋯⋯⋯⋯⋯⋯⋯⋯⋯⋯	153
		Section 1 Listening ⋯⋯⋯⋯⋯⋯⋯⋯⋯⋯⋯⋯⋯⋯⋯⋯⋯⋯	153
		Section 2 Watching ⋯⋯⋯⋯⋯⋯⋯⋯⋯⋯⋯⋯⋯⋯⋯⋯⋯⋯	153
	Part Two	Reading and Writing ⋯⋯⋯⋯⋯⋯⋯⋯⋯⋯⋯⋯⋯⋯⋯⋯⋯⋯⋯	154
		Text A Amusing Ourselves to Death ⋯⋯⋯⋯⋯⋯⋯⋯⋯⋯	154
	Part Three	Reading and Speaking ⋯⋯⋯⋯⋯⋯⋯⋯⋯⋯⋯⋯⋯⋯⋯⋯⋯	162
		Text B Always On: Personal and Cognitive Consequences ⋯	162
	Part Four	Cross Cultural Communication ⋯⋯⋯⋯⋯⋯⋯⋯⋯⋯⋯⋯⋯⋯	167
		Passage A 微博"意见领袖"的影响力 ⋯⋯⋯⋯⋯⋯⋯⋯⋯⋯	167
		Passage B Five Types of Social Media Influencers ⋯⋯⋯⋯⋯	168

Unit 1

LANGUAGE AND LITERATURE

That is part of the beauty of all literature. You discover that your longings are universal longings, that you're not lonely and isolated from anyone. You belong.

—By F. Scott Fitzgerald

Learning Objectives

Upon completion of this unit, you should be able to:

Remember & Understand	★ recognize and recite the key terms and well-known lines of the chosen literature in this unit; ★ summarize in your own words the thesis and the major points of Text A and Text B;
Analyze & Apply	★ use root to better understand a new word and enlarge vocabulary; ★ make reference to the thesis and/or the major points of Text A and Text B in your writing; ★ use participles to rewrite the given sentences;
Evaluate & Create	★ incorporate prepositions in descriptive paragraphs; ★ synthesize information about literature versus life; ★ deliver a clear and coherent oral presentation on your chosen book and list the reasons why you love it.

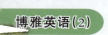

Part One Lead-in

Section 1 Listening

Task 1 Filling in the Blanks

Directions: Please fill in the blanks with words or sentences on the basis of what you have heard.

A Psalm of Life

—Henry Wadsworth Longfellow

(What the Heart of the Yours Man Said to the Psalmist.)
Tell me not, in mournful numbers,
_____1_____!
for the soul is dead that slumbers,
And things are not what they seem.

_____2_____!
And the grave is not its goal;
"Dust thou art, to dust returnest,"
Was not spoken of the soul.

Not enjoyment, and ___3___,
Is our destined end or way;
But to act, that each to-morrow
Find us ___4___ than to-day.

Art is long, and Time is fleeting,
And our hearts, though stout and brave,
Still, like muffled drums, are ___5___
Funeral marches to the grave.

In the world's broad field of battle,
In the bivouac of Life,
Be not like dumb, driven cattle!
_____6_____!

Trust no future, howe'er pleasant!
Let the dead Past bury its dead!
Act, — _____7_____!
Heart within, and God o'erhead!

Lives of great men all remind us
We can make our lives ___8___,
And, departing, leave behind us
Footprints on the sands of time;

Footprints, that perhaps another,
Sailing o'er life's solemn main,
A forlorn and shipwrecked brother,
Seeing, shall ___9___ again.

Let us, then, be up and doing,
With a heart for any fate;
Still achieving, still pursuing,
_____10_____.

Task 2 Reciting and Group Discussion

Directions: Please recite the first three stanzas of the poem and discuss the following questions in pairs or groups.

1. Do you agree with the line in the poem — "Life is but an empty dream!"?
2. Discuss with your pairs about the theme of this poem.

Section 2 Watching

Task 1 Answer the following questions

Directions: Please watch the video "How Books Open Our Mind" and answer the following questions.

1. List some of the books she read and the benefits she got from reading.
2. What is the first book she read in the US? And what is it about?
3. What did she get from comparative reading?

Task 2 Discussion

Directions: Please discuss the following questions in pairs or groups.

1. Do you love reading? If so, please list some of the books that you have read.
2. Francis Bacon ever put it — "Studies serves for delight, for ornament and for ability." Do you agree or disagree?
3. What are your personal benefits from reading?

Part Two Reading and Writing

Text A

The Autobiography of Benjamin Franklin
(Excerpt)
Benjamin Franklin

1   Then I walked up the street, gazing about till near the market-house I met a boy with bread. I had made many a meal on bread, and, *inquiring* where he got it, I went immediately to the baker's he directed me to, in Second-street, and ask'd for bisket, intending such as we had in Boston; but they, it seems, were not made in Philadelphia. Then I asked for a three-penny loaf, and was told they had none such. So not considering or knowing the difference of money, and the greater cheapness nor the names of his bread, I made him give me three-penny worth of any sort. He gave me, accordingly, three great puffy rolls. I was surprised at the quantity, but took it, and, having no room in my pockets, walk'd off with a roll under each arm, and eating the other.

2   Thus I went up Market-street as far as Fourth-street, passing by the door of Mr. Read, my future wife's father; when she, standing at the door, saw me, and thought I made, as I certainly did, a most *awkward*, *ridiculous* appearance. Then I turned and went down Chestnut-street and part of Walnut-street, eating my roll all the way, and, corning round, found myself again at Market-street wharf, near the boat I came in, to which I went for a *draught* of the river water; and, being filled with one of my rolls, gave the other two to a woman and her child that came down the river in the boat with us, and were waiting to go farther.

3   Thus refreshed, I walked again up the street, which by this time had many clean-dressed people in it, who were all walking the same way. I joined them, and thereby was led into the great meeting-house of *the Quakers* near the market. I sat down among them, and, after looking round awhile and hearing nothing said, being very *drowsy* thro' labor and want of rest the *preceding* night, I *fell fast asleep*, and continued so till the meeting *broke up*, when one was kind enough to rouse me. This was, therefore, the first house I was in, or slept in, in Philadelphia.

4   After dinner, my sleepiness return'd, and being shown to a bed, I lay down without undressing, and slept till six in the evening, was call'd to supper, went to bed again very early, and slept soundly till next morning. Then I made myself as tidy as I could, and went to Andrew Bradford the printer's. I found in the shop the old man his father, whom I had seen at New York, and who, travelling on horseback, had got to Philadelphia before me. He introduced me to his son, who receiv'd me *civilly*, gave me

a breakfast, but told me he did not at present want a hand, being lately suppli'd with one; but there was another printer in town, lately set up, one Keimer, who, perhaps, might employ me.

The old gentleman said he would go with me to the new printer; and when we found him, "Neighbor," says Bradford, "I have brought to see you a young man of your business; perhaps you may want such a one." He ask'd me a few questions, put a composing stick in my hand to see how I work'd, and then said he would employ me soon, though he had just then nothing for me to do; and, taking old Bradford, whom he had never seen before, to be one of the town's people that had a good will for him, enter'd into a conversation on his present undertaking and projects. I, who stood by and heard all, saw immediately that one of them was a *crafty* old *sophister*, and the other a mere *novice*. Bradford left me with Keimer, who was greatly surpris'd when I told him who the old man was.

I began now to have some acquaintance among the young people of the town, that were lovers of reading, with whom I spent my evenings very pleasantly; and gaining money by my *industry* and *frugality*, I lived very agreeably, forgetting Boston as much as I could. *At length*, an incident happened that sent me back again much sooner than I had intended. I had a brother-in-law, Robert Holmes, master of a *sloop* that traded between Boston and Delaware. He being at Newcastle, forty miles below Philadelphia, heard there of me, and wrote me a letter mentioning the concern of my friends in Boston at my *abrupt departure*, *assuring me of* their good will to me, and that everything would be accommodated to my mind if I would return, to which he exhorted me very earnestly. I wrote an answer to his letter, thank'd him for his advice, but stated my reasons for quitting Boston fully and in such a light as to convince him I was not so wrong as he had apprehended.

Sir William Keith, governor of the province, was then at Newcastle, and Captain Holmes, happening to be in company with him when my letter came to hand, spoke to him of me, and show'd him the letter. The governor read it, and seem'd surpris'd when he was told my age. He said I appear'd a young man of promising parts, and therefore should be encouraged; the printers at Philadelphia were *wretched* ones; and, if I would set up there, he made no doubt I should succeed; for his part, he would *procure* me the public business, and do me every other service in his power. This my brother-in-law afterwards told me in Boston, but I knew as yet nothing of it; when, one day, Keimer and I being at work together near the window, we saw the governor and another gentleman, finely dress'd, come directly across the street to our house, and heard them at the door.

Keimer ran down immediately, thinking it a visit to him; but the governor inquir'd for me, came up, and with a *condescension* of politeness I had been quite unus'd to, made me many *compliments*, desired to *be acquainted with* me, blam'd me kindly for not having made myself known to him when I first came to the place, and would have me away with him to the tavern. I went, however, with the governor and *Colonel* French to a *tavern*, at the corner of Third-street, and over the Madeira he propos'd my setting up my business, laid before me the probabilities of success, and both he and Colonel French assur'd me I should have their interest and influence in procuring the public business of both governments. On my doubting whether my father would assist me in it, Sir William said he would give me a letter to him, in which he would state the advantages, and he did not doubt of *prevailing* with him.

(1149 words)

New Words

inquire	[ɪnˈkwaɪə]	v.	to ask for information 询问,打听
awkward	[ˈɔːkwəd]	a.	embarrassing and not relaxed 尴尬的,笨拙的
ridiculous	[rɪˈdɪkjʊləs]	a.	stupid or unreasonable and deserving to be laughed at 愚蠢的,可笑的
draught	[drɑːft]	n.	a current of unpleasantly cold air/water blowing through 气流,水流
drowsy	[ˈdraʊzi]	a.	being in a state between sleeping and being awake 睡意朦胧的
precede	[prɪˈsiːd]	v.	to be or go before sth. or sb. in time or space 处于……之前
civilly	[ˈsɪvɪli]	ad.	in a polite way 有礼貌地
crafty	[ˈkrɑːfti]	a.	clever, esp. in a dishonest or secret way 狡猾的
sophister	[ˈsɒfɪstə]	n.	a person who is clever in a complicated and shrewd way 精明的人
novice	[ˈnɒvɪs]	n.	a person who is not experienced in a job or situation 新手
industry	[ˈɪndəstri]	n.	the quality of regularly working hard 勤奋
frugality	[fruːˈɡæləti]	n.	quality of being careful when using money or food, or (of a meal) cheap or small in amount 简朴,节约
sloop	[sluːp]	n.	a small sailing boat with one mast 单桅帆船
abrupt	[əˈbrʌpt]	a.	sudden and unexpected, and often unpleasant 突然的
departure	[dɪˈpɑːtʃər]	n.	the fact of a person or vehicle, etc. leaving somewhere 离开
exhort	[ɪɡˈzɔːt]	v.	to strongly encourage or try to persuade sb. to do sth. 激励,敦促
wretched	[ˈretʃɪd]	a.	very bad or of poor quality 糟糕的,可怜的
procure	[prəˈkjʊər]	v.	to get sth., esp. after an effort 取得,获得
condescension	[ˌkɒndɪˈsenʃən]	n.	affability to your inferiors and temporary disregard for differences of position or rank 屈尊
compliment	[ˈkɒmplɪmənt]	n.	a remark that expresses approval, admiration, or respect 恭维,赞扬
colonel	[ˈkɜːnəl]	n.	an officer of high rank in the army or air force 上校

Unit 1

tavern	[ˈtævən]	*n.*	a place where alcohol is sold and drunk 小酒馆
prevail	[prɪˈveɪl]	*v.*	to get control or influence 占优势，占上风

Phrases and Expressions

fall fast asleep	to start to sleep soundly 熟睡
break up	to come to the end 结束，解散
at length	at last 最后，终于
assure sb. of	to tell someone confidently that sth. is true, esp. so that they do not worry 向……保证
be acquainted with	to know or be familiar with a person 与……结识

Proper Noun

the Quaker	a member of a Christian group called the Society of Friends, which does not have formal ceremonies or a formal system of beliefs, and which is strongly opposed to violence and war 贵格会教徒

Notes

1. The text was an abridged excerpt from Chapter 3 of *The Autobiography of Benjamin Franklin*. The autobiography is an unfinished record of his own life, written from 1771 to 1790, four parts in total. The first English edition was published after his death in 1793. As one of the most famous and influential examples of autobiography ever, it is a simple yet faithful, immensely fascinating account of a man rising to wealth and fame from a state of poverty and obscurity, which became the prototype of the American Dream. In terms of language, it is plain in style, homely in imagery, and simple in diction as well as syntax.

2. Benjamin Franklin (1706—1790) was one of the Founding Fathers of the United States and in many ways was "the First American." As a renowned polymath, Franklin was a leading author, printer, political theorist, politician, postmaster, scientist, inventor, civic activist, statesman, and diplomat. He was the only American who once signed all the four monumental documents: the Declaration of Independence (1776), the Constitution of the United States (1787), the Federalist Papers (1787—1788) and the Bill of Rights (1791). He demonstrated all the major principles of the Enlightenment in America. He embodied the transition from Puritan piety, idealism and provincialism to the more secular, utilitarian and cosmopolitan values of the American Enlightenment.

Task 1   Generating the Outline

Directions: Please identify the main point of each paragraph. You may use the table below to help you.

Para. 1	Purchasing _____ upon the first arrival of the new city.
Para. 2	First glimpse of his _____ while roaming in the street and eating the bread awkwardly.
Para. 3	A sound sleep in the meeting house of _____ due to labor and lack of sleep the previous night.
Para. 4	Looking for employment firstly at _____.
Para. 5	Being accompanied to a new printer at _____ and acquired the personalities of Bradford and Keimer.
Para. 6	Settling down in Philadelphia and receiving the letter from _____.
Para. 7	_____ good impression on me via his brother-in-law's introduction.
Para. 8	Governor's unexpected visit to me and _____ to set up my own business.

Task 2   Understanding the Text

Directions: Please answer the following questions based on Text A.

1. Please describe the scene of bread purchasing in your own words.
2. What was the author like when he was passing his future wife's door?
3. What does "this" refer to in the sentence — "This was, therefore, the first house I was in, or slept in, in Philadelphia."? (Para. 3)
4. How was the author received in Andrew Bradford the printer's?
5. According to the author's observation, what kind of people were Bradford and Keimer?
6. How did the author get along with the young people in Philadelphia?
7. What was the governor's impression on the author after his brother-in-law spoke of the author and showed the governor the author's letter?
8. Please describe the scene of the governor's first visit to the author.
9. What did the governor propose to the author in the tavern and what was the author's doubt?

Task 3   Vocabulary Building

Directions: Please identify the meanings of the roots and guess the meanings of the words with the same root.

> quir/ quis/ quer/ quest = seek, search;   ced/ ceed/ cess = go, move;
> nov = new;   rupt = break;   scend/ scens/ scent = climb

1. **quir/ quis/ quer/ quest = seek, search** 表示"寻求,询问"

     acquire   v.   获取(ac 加强动作+quire 寻求得到→获取)

Unit 1

acquired	a.	后天习得的(acquire+ed)
acquirement	n.	获得,学识(acquire+ment)
acquisitive	a.	贪得无厌的(ac不断+quis+itive→不断寻求→贪得无厌的)
conquer	v.	征服(con全部+quer→全部寻求到→征服)
conquest	n.	征服(con+quest)
inquire	v.	盘问,追究(in进入+quire→问进去→盘问)
inquisition	n.	调查,审问(in进入+quis+ition→进去问→调查)
inquest	n.	审问(in进+quest→问进去→审问)
prerequisite	n.	先决条件(pre预先+requisite必需品→先决条件)
quest	n.	探求,寻找
question	n.	疑问(quest+ion)
request	v./n.	要求,恳请(re再+quest→再寻求→要求)
require	v.	请求,命令(re再+quire→再寻求→请求)
requisite	a./n.	必要的,(re再+quis+ite→一再寻求→必要的);必需品

2. ced/ ceed/ cess = go, move 表示"走,移动"

antecede	v.	先行,先于(ante前+cede→走在前面→先行)

3. nov=new 表示"新的"

innovate	v.	革新,改革(in进入+nov+ate)

4. rupt = break 表示"断裂"

abrupt	a.	突然的(ab离开+rupt→断开→突然断开→突然的)

5. scend/ scens/ scent = climb 表示"爬,攀登"

ascend	v.	登上,爬上(a向上+scend)

Task 4 Learning Phrases

Directions: Please fill in the blanks in the sentences below with the phrases listed in the box. Change the forms if necessary. Notice that some phrases need to be used more than once.

fall fast asleep	*break up*	*at length*	*assure sb of*
be acquainted with	*happen to*	*blame sb for*	*have a good will for sb*

1. _____, Captain Ahab darted his harpoon into Moby Dick, however, the rope caught him round the neck and he sunk into the sea with the white whale voicelessly.
2. Rip Van Winkle _____ in the mountain for decades after drinking some moonshine from a group of people with antiquated Dutch clothing.
3. Miss Watson is hard on Huck, and she often _____ him _____ his "uncivilized" behavior.
4. Widow Douglas, who _____ Huck, always tries her best to civilize Huck, believing that it

is her Christian duty.

5. The friendship between Fredric Nietzsche and Richard Wagner _____ because of Nietzsche's relentless criticism on Wagner's works.

6. The disabled Chinese poet Yu Xiuhua _____ become extremely popular after one of her poems was published by a poetry magazine on WeChat and she has even been identified as "Chinese Emily Dickson."

7. Fortunately, Benjamin Franklin _____ the governors of Pennsylvania and New York State when he was still a teenager.

8. Cormac McCarthy describes the violent scenes _____ in his novel Blood Meridian, that is, he displays so many details about hurting and killing which make most readers feel uncomfortable.

9. Herman Melville _____ Nathanial Hawthorne in a friend's party and a great friendship was developed since then.

10. Woodrow Wilson _____ the enthusiastic young people _____ the fact that WWI would be a war that ended all wars, however, the disillusioned promise partially led to the Lost Generation in the 1920s.

Task 5 Studying the Sentence Structure
Participles
Sentences from the text

1. Then I walked up the street, *gazing* about till near the market-house I met a boy with bread. I had made many a meal on bread, and, *inquiring* where he got it, I went immediately to the baker's he directed me to, in Second-street, and ask'd for bisket, *intending* such as we had in Boston. (Para. 1).

2. Thus *refreshed*, I walked again up the street, which by this time had many clean-dressed people in it, who were all walking the same way. (Para. 3).

3. I sat down among them, and, after looking round awhile and hearing nothing said, being very drowsy thro' labor and want of rest the *preceding* night, I fell fast asleep, and continued so till the meeting broke up, when one was kind enough to rouse me. (Para. 3)

4. We saw the governor and another gentleman, finely *dress'd*, come directly across the street to our house, and heard them at the door. (Para. 7)

Directions: Please rewrite the following sentences by using participles.

1. A green and yellow parrot, which hung in a cage outside the door, kept repeating over and over "Allez vous-en! Allez vous-en! Sapristi! That's all right!"

_____
_____
_____

2. Mr. Pontellier finally lit a cigar and began to smoke, letting the paper drag idly from his hand. He fixed his gaze upon a white sunshade that was advancing at snail's pace from the beach.

_____

3. He was already acquainted with the market reports, and he glanced restlessly over the editorials and bits of news which he had not had time to read before quitting New Orleans the day before.

Task 6 Paraphrasing Difficult Sentences

1. Thus I went up Market-street as far as Fourth-street, passing by the door of Mr. Read, my future wife's father; when she, standing at the door, saw me, and thought I made, as I certainly did, a most awkward, ridiculous appearance.

2. Being very drowsy thro' labor and want of rest the preceding night, I fell fast asleep, and continued so till the meeting broke up, when one was kind enough to rouse me.

3. I, who stood by and heard all, saw immediately that one of them was a crafty old sophister, and the other a mere novice.

4. He being at Newcastle, forty miles below Philadelphia, heard there of me, and wrote me a letter mentioning the concern of my friends in Boston at my abrupt departure, assuring me of their good will to me, and that everything would be accommodated to my mind if I would return, to which he exhorted me very earnestly.

5. Keimer ran down immediately, thinking it a visit to him; but the governor inquir'd for me, came up, and with a condescension of politeness I had been quite unus'd to, made me many compliments, desired to be acquainted with me, blam'd me kindly for not having made myself known to him when I first came to the place, and would have me away with him to the tavern.

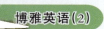

Task 7　Summarizing the Text

Directions: Please summarize Text A with approximately 200 words. You may use the table in Task 1 to help you.

_____
_____
_____
_____
_____
_____
_____

Task 8　Describing a Place

Directions: Write a passage to describe the physical environment of a place, such as a place of interest or a familiar setting around you.

Tips

1. Proper use of prepositions.
2. Pay attention to how the place is organized.

Part Three　Reading and Speaking

Text B

Why Do We Read Fiction?
(Excerpt)
Robert Penn Warren

1　　Why do we read *fiction*? The answer is simple. We read it because we like it. And we like it because fiction, as an image of life, *stimulates* and *gratifies* our interest in life. But whatever interests may be appealed to by fiction, the special and immediate interest that takes us to fiction is always our interest in a story.

2　　The story promises us a *resolution*, and we wait in suspense to learn how things will *come out*. We are in *suspense*, not only about what will happen, but even more about what the event will mean. We are in suspense about the story in fiction because we are in suspense about another story far closer and more important to us—the story of our own life as we live it. We do not know how that story of our own life is going to come out. We do not know what it will mean. So, in that deepest suspense of life, which will be shadowed in the suspense we feel about the story in fiction, we turn to fiction for some slight *hint* about the story in the life we live. The relation of our life to the fictional life is what, in a *fundamental* sense, takes us to fiction.

Even when we read, as we say, to "escape," we seek to escape not from life but to life, to a life more satisfying than our own *drab* version. Fiction gives us an image of life—sometimes of a life we actually have and like to dwell on, but often and *poignantly* of one we have had but do not have now, or one we have never had and can never have. The little *coed*, worrying about her *snub nose* and her low mark in Sociology, dreams of being a *debutante* out of F. Scott Fitzgerald; and the thin-chested freshman, still troubled by *acne*, dreams of being a granite-jawed Neanderthal out of Mickey Spillane.

And that is what fiction in one sense, is—a daydream. It is, in other words, an imaginative enactment. In it we find, in imagination, not only the pleasure of recognizing the world we know and of reliving our past, but also the pleasure of entering worlds we do not know and of experimenting with experiences which we deeply crave but which the limitations of life, the fear of consequences, or the severity of our principles forbid to us. Fiction can give us this pleasure without any painful consequences, for there is no price tag on the magic world of imaginative enactment. But fiction does not give us only what we want; more importantly, it may give us things we hadn't even known we wanted.

How often have we heard some *sentimental* old lady says of a book: "I just loved the heroine —I mean I just went through everything with her and I knew exactly how she felt. Then when she died I just cried." The sweet old lady, even if she isn't very *sophisticated*, is *instinctively* playing a double game: She *identifies herself with* the heroine, but she survives the heroine's death to shed the delicious tears. So even the old lady knows how to make the most of what we shall call her role taking. She knows that doubleness, in the very act of identification, is of the essence of role taking: there is the taker of the role and there is the role taken. And fiction is, in imaginative enactment, a role taking.

But all along the way, role taking leads us, *by the same token*, to an awareness of ourselves; it leads us, in fact, to the creation of the self. All our *submerged* selves, the old desires and possibilities, are *lurking* deep in us, sleepless and eager to have another go. Fiction, most often in subtly disguised forms, liberatingly reenacts for us such inner conflict. We feel the pleasure of liberation even when we cannot specify the source of the pleasure.

When in Thackeray's *Vanity Fair* the girl Becky Sharp, leaving school for good, tosses her copy of Dr. Johnson's Dictionary out of the carriage, something in our own heart leaps gaily up, just as something *rejoices* at her later sexual and *pecuniary* adventures in Victorian society, and suffers, against all our sense of moral justice, when she *comes a cropper*. When we read Dostoevsky's *Crime and Punishment*, something in our nature participates in the bloody deed, and later, something else in us experiences, with the murdered Raskolnikov, the bliss of *repentance* and *reconciliation*.

We feel, in the end, some sense of reconciliation with the world and with ourselves. And this process of moving through conflict to reconciliation is an echo of our own life process. The life process, as we know it from babyhood on, from our early relations with our parents on to our adult relation with the world, is a long process of conflict and reconciliation. This process of enriching and deepening experience is a pattern of *oscillation*—a pattern resembling that of the lovers' quarrel: when lovers quarrel, each asserts his special ego against that of the beloved and then in the moment of making up finds more keenly than before the joy of losing the self in the love of another. So in fiction we enter imaginatively a situation of difficulty and estrangement—a *problematic* situation that, as we said earlier, sharpens our awareness of life—and move through it to a reconciliation which seems fresh and sweet.

(915 words)

New Words

fiction	[ˈfɪkʃən]	n.	the type of book or story that is written about imaginary characters and events and not based on real people and facts 小说
stimulate	[ˈstɪmjʊleɪt]	v.	to make someone excited and interested about sth. 激发，刺激
gratify	[ˈgrætɪfaɪ]	v.	to please someone, or to satisfy a wish or need 使满足
resolution	[ˌrezəˈluːʃən]	n.	a promise to yourself to do or not do sth. 决定
suspense	[səˈspens]	n.	the feeling of excitement or nervousness that you have when you are waiting for sth. to happen and are uncertain about what it is going to be 焦虑，悬念
hint	[hɪnt]	n.	sth. that you say or do that shows, but not directly, what you think or want 暗示
fundamental	[ˌfʌndəˈmentəl]	a.	forming the base, from which everything else develops 基本的，主要的
drab	[dræb]	a.	boring, esp. in appearance; having little color and excitement 单调的，乏味的
poignantly	[ˈpɔɪnjəntli]	ad.	causing or having a very sharp feeling of sadness 令人痛苦地
coed	[ˌkəʊˈed]	n.	a female student in a college with male and female students 男女合校的女生
debutante	[ˈdebjuːtɒnt]	n.	a rich young woman who, esp. in the past in Britain, went to a number of social events as a way

Unit 1

			of being introduced to other young people of high social rank 上流社会的年轻女子
acne	[ˈækni]	n.	a skin disease common in young people, in which small, red spots appear on the face and neck 粉刺，痤疮
sentimental	[ˌsentɪˈmentəl]	a.	too strongly influenced by emotional feelings 多愁善感的
sophisticated	[səˈfɪstɪkeɪtɪd]	a.	clever in a complicated way and therefore able to do complicated tasks 老练的，精于世故的
instinctively	[ɪnˈstɪŋktɪvli]	ad.	not thought about, planned or developed by training 本能的，直觉的
submerge	[səbˈmɜːdʒ]	v.	to go below or make sth. go below the surface of the sea or a river or lake 浸没，淹没
lurk	[lɜːk]	v.	to wait or move in a secret way so that you cannot be seen, esp. because you are about to attack someone or do sth. wrong 潜伏，隐藏
rejoice	[rɪˈdʒɔɪs]	v.	to feel or show great happiness about sth. 非常高兴，非常欣喜
pecuniary	[pɪˈkjuːnjəri]	a.	relating to money 金钱上的
repentance	[rɪˈpentəns]	n.	to be very sorry for sth. bad you have done in the past and wish that you had not done it 忏悔
reconciliation	[ˌrekənˌsɪliˈeɪʃən]	n.	a situation in which two people or groups of people become friendly again after they have argued 和解，和好
oscillation	[ˌɒsɪˈleɪʃən]	n.	moving repeatedly from one position to another 振荡
problematic	[ˌprɒbləˈmætɪk]	a.	full of problems or difficulties 有问题的

 Phrases & Expressions

come out	sth. becomes known publicly after it has been kept secret 揭秘真相
snub nose	a nose that is short and turns upwards at the end 塌鼻子，狮子鼻
identify oneself with	to believe that someone or sth. is closely connected or involved with sth. 认为与……密切相关
by the same token	used to mean that sth. you are about to say is also true, for the same reasons as what has just been 同样地
come a cropper	to fail badly, or to fall from a horse or have a bad accident in a vehicle 陷入困境，跌落

15

 **Notes**

1. This passage is an abridged excerpt from the essay "Why Do We Read Fiction" by Robert Penn Warren.
2. Robert Penn Warren (April 24, 1905—September 15, 1989) was an American poet, novelist, and literary critic and was one of the founders of New Criticism. He was also a charter member of the Fellowship of Southern Writers. He founded the influential literary journal *The Southern Review* with Cleanth Brooks in 1935. He received the 1947 Pulitzer Prize for his novel *All the King's Men* (1946) and the Pulitzer Prize for Poetry in 1958 and 1979. He is the only person who won Pulitzer Prizes for both fiction and poetry.

Task 1   Structure Mind-Mapping

Directions: Go over the text and complete the structure information by filling the gaps.

Mind Mapping	Details
Thesis: Fiction stimulates and gratifies our _____.	The special and immediate interest that takes us to fiction is always our _____.
Point 1: Reading fiction for _____	We wait in suspense to learn how the story in fiction and _____ will come out.
Point 2: Reading fiction as day-dreaming	We escape to life to find the pleasure of recognizing the familiar world and _____ for various reasons.
Point 3: Reading fiction as _____	We identify ourselves with _____ of the story, subsequently awakening the dormant selves and feeling the pleasure of liberation.
Point 4: Reading fiction as _____ with the world and oneself	The process from conflict to reconciliation echoes _____.

Task 2   Synthesizing Information

Directions: The audio clip and the video clip in Part One, Text A, and Text B are all about literature/ books versus life. Please work in groups to complete the table below, summarizing the function of literature/ books on life. An example is already done for you. Please report the results of your group to the class.

Sources	Functions
Audio clip — "A Psalm of Life"	Literature _____ life.
Video clip —"How Books Open Our Mind"	Books /literature _____ life.

Text A—"The Autobiography of Benjamin Franklin"	Literature _____ life.
Text B—"Why Do We Read Fiction"	Literature _____ life.

Task 3   Making Presentation

Directions: Please choose one of the following novels as your topic and give an oral presentation on why you like reading this novel.

The Great Gatsby by F. Scott Fitzgerald
Jane Eyre by Charlotte Brontë
The Old Man and the Sea by Earnest Hemingway
On the Road by Jack Kerouac

Tips

1. Summarize the plot of the chosen novel briefly.
2. You may identify yourself with one of the characters in the novel or other aspects that impressed you.
3. You are supposed to cite at least two textual references to justify your reasons.

Part Four   Cross Cultural Communication

Passage A

许渊冲翻译理论的中国特色

2014年8月2日,在第二十届世界翻译大会会员代表大会上,由中国翻译协会推荐的我国著名英、法语文学翻译家、外国文学研究专家、翻译文化终身成就奖获得者、北京大学新闻与传播学院许渊冲教授荣获国际译界最高奖项之一——2014"北极光"杰出文学翻译奖,成为该奖项1999年设立以来,第一位获此殊荣的亚洲翻译家。国际译联杰出文学翻译奖评审委员会对许渊冲教授的颁奖词称:"我们所处的国际化环境需要富有成效的交流,许渊冲教授一直致力于为使用汉语、英语和法语的人们建立起沟通的桥梁。"

——题记

努力从中国文化本身的传统来总结翻译理论,是许渊冲翻译理论的重要特点。我把文学翻译总结为"美化之艺术",就是三美(意美、音美、形美),三化(等化、浅化、深化),三之(知之、好之、乐之)的艺术。其中三美是诗词翻译的本体论,三化是方法论,三之是目的论,艺术是认识论。这样的表达非常中国化,但这样的表达确是许渊冲先生从中国文化本身汲取营养所做的创造性转化。"三美"之说来源于鲁迅,鲁迅在《汉文学史纲要》中指出:"诵习一字,当识形音义三:口诵耳闻其音,目察其形,心通其义,三识并用,一字之功乃全。其在文章,则写山曰嶙峋嵯峨,状水曰汪洋澎湃,蔽芾葱茏,恍逢丰木,鳟鲂鳗鲤,如见多鱼。故其所函,遂具三美:意美以感心,一也;音美以感耳,二也;形美以感目,三也。"1978年,许渊冲在自己翻译的《毛泽东诗词四十二首》英文、法文版的序言中正式把鲁迅的这个观点运用到对中国古代诗歌的外译上,提出了"三美"理论。许渊冲的"三之"理论也是从中国文化中提取出来的。孔子在《论语·雍也》中说:"知之者不如好之者,好之者不如乐之者。"

许渊冲翻译理论中最具有特色和创造性的是他从《易经》中所汲取的智慧,总结出的翻译理论。他所提出的译者八论,极有智慧,他说:"翻译学也可以说是《易经》,'换易语言'之经;自然,译学的八论和《易经》的八卦是形同实异的,现在解释如下:一论:译者一也,译文应该在字句、篇章、文化的层次和原文统一。二论:译者依也,译文只能以原文字句为依据。三论:译者异也,译文可以创新立异。一至三论是翻译的方法论。四论:译者易也,翻译要换易语言形式。五论:译者意也,翻译要传情达意,包括言内之情,言外之意。六论:译者艺也,文学翻译是艺术,不是科学。四至六论是翻译的认识论,也可以算是'译者依也'的补论。七论:译者益也,翻译要能开卷有益,使人'知之'。八论:译者怡也,文学翻译要能怡性悦情,使人'好之'、'乐之'。七八论是翻译的目的论。"

许渊冲套用《道德经》的语言所总结的翻译理论,在语言上达到了炉火纯青的地步,在理论上也完备而简洁,这是近百年来中国学者对翻译理论的最精彩总结。

译可译,非常译。
忘其形,得其意。
得意,理解之始;
忘形,表达之母。
故应得意,以求其同;
故可忘形,以存其异。
两者同出,异名同理。
得意忘形,求同存异;
翻译之道。

(1173字)

 注解

1. 本篇节选改编自张西平的文章《许渊冲——中国古代文化翻译的探索者》。该文载于2014年6月25日《中华读书报》。
2. 作者张西平系北京外国语大学教授,北京外国语大学海外汉学研究中心主任、博士生导师。

Directions: Please read the Chinese classical poem below translated by Xu Yuanchong and finish the following tasks.

1. Identify the Chinese version of this poem.
2. Appreciate the poem based on Xu's theory of translation.

Autumn Thoughts

Translated by Xu Yuanchong

Over old trees
Wreathed with rotten vines fly evening crows;
Under a small bridge near a cottage a stream flows;
On ancient road in the west wind a lean horse goes.
Westward declines the sun;
Far, far away home is the heartbroken one.

Passage B

Tradition and the Individual Talent
T.S. Eliot

No poet, no artist of any art, has his complete meaning alone. His significance, his appreciation is the appreciation of his relation to the dead poets and artists. You cannot value him alone; you must set him, for contrast and comparison, among the dead. I mean this as a principle of aesthetic, not merely historical, criticism. The necessity that he shall conform, that he shall cohere, is not one-sided; what happens when a new work of art is created is something that happens simultaneously to all the works of art which preceded it. The existing monuments form an ideal order among themselves, which is modified by the introduction of the new (the really new) work of art among them. The existing order is complete before the new work arrives; for order to persist after the supervention of novelty, the whole existing order must be, if ever so slightly, altered; and so the relations, proportions, values of each work of art toward the whole are readjusted; and this is conformity between the old and the new. Whoever has approved this idea of order, of the form of European, of English literature, will not find it preposterous that the past should be altered by the present as much as the present is directed by the past. And the poet who is aware of this will be aware of great difficulties and responsibilities.

In a peculiar sense he will be aware also that he must inevitably be judged by the standards of the past. I say judged, not amputated, by them; not judged to be as good as, or worse or better than, the dead; and certainly not judged by the canons of dead critics. It is a judgment, a comparison, in which two things are measured by each other. To conform merely would be for the new work not really to conform at all; it would not be new, and would therefore not be a work of art. And we do not quite say that the new is more valuable because it fits in; but its fitting in is a test of its value—a test, it is true, which can only be slowly and cautiously applied, for we are none of us infallible judges of conformity. We say: it appears to conform, and is perhaps individual, or it appears individual, and may conform; but we are hardly likely to find that it is one and not the other.

To proceed to a more intelligible exposition of the relation of the poet to the past: he can neither take the past as a lump, an indiscriminate bolus, nor can he form himself wholly on one or two private admirations, nor can he form himself wholly upon one preferred period. The first course is inadmissible, the second is an important experience of youth, and the third is a pleasant and highly desirable supplement. The poet must be very conscious of the main current, which does not at all flow invariably through the most distinguished reputations. He must be quite aware of the obvious fact that art never improves, but that the material of art is never quite the same. He must be aware that the mind of Europe—the mind of his own country—a mind which he learns in time to be much more important than his own private mind—is a mind which changes, and that this change is a development which abandons nothing en route, which does not superannuate either Shakespeare, or Homer, or the rock drawing of the Magdalenian draughtsmen. That this development, refinement perhaps, complication certainly, is not, from the point of view of the artist, any improvement. Perhaps not even an improvement from the point of view of the psychologist or not to the extent which we imagine; perhaps only in the end based upon a complication in economics and machinery. But the difference between the present and the past is that the

conscious present is an awareness of the past in a way and to an extent which the past's awareness of itself cannot show.

Some one said: "The dead writers are remote from us because we know so much more than they did." Precisely, and they are that which we know.

I am alive to a usual objection to what is clearly part of my programme for the métier of poetry. The objection is that the doctrine requires a ridiculous amount of erudition (pedantry), a claim which can be rejected by appeal to the lives of poets in any pantheon. It will even be affirmed that much learning deadens or perverts poetic sensibility. While, however, we persist in believing that a poet ought to know as much as will not encroach upon his necessary receptivity and necessary laziness, it is not desirable to confine knowledge to whatever can be put into a useful shape for examinations, drawing-rooms, or the still more pretentious modes of publicity. Some can absorb knowledge, the more tardy must sweat for it. Shakespeare acquired more essential history from Plutarch than most men could from the whole British Museum. What is to be insisted upon is that the poet must develop or procure the consciousness of the past and that he should continue to develop this consciousness throughout his career.

What happens is a continual surrender of himself as he is at the moment to something which is more valuable. The progress of an artist is a continual self-sacrifice, a continual extinction of personality.

There remains to define this process of depersonalization and its relation to the sense of tradition. It is in this depersonalization that art may be said to approach the condition of science. I shall, therefore, invite you to consider, as a suggestive analogy, the action which takes place when a bit of finely filiated platinum is introduced into a chamber containing oxygen and sulphur dioxide.

(979 words)

1. The passage was adapted from "Tradition and the Individual Talent" by T.S. Eliot, composed in 1919.
2. Thomas Stearns Eliot (26 September, 1888—4 January, 1965), better known as T. S. Eliot, was an essayist, publisher, playwright, literary and social critic. He was born in St. Louis, Missouri and emigrated to England in 1914 (at age 25), settling, working and marrying there. He was eventually naturalized as a British subject in 1927 at age 39, renouncing his American citizenship. Eliot attracted widespread attention for his poem *The Love Song of J. Alfred Prufrock* (1915), which is seen as a masterpiece of the Modernist movement. It was followed by some of the best-known poems in the English language, including *The Waste Land* (1922), *The Hollow Men* (1925), *Ash Wednesday* (1930), and *Four Quartets* (1945). He is also known for his seven plays, particularly *Murder in the Cathedral* (1935). He was awarded the Nobel Prize in Literature in 1948, "for his outstanding, pioneer contribution to present-day poetry."

Directions: Please summarize the passage in Chinese. Your summary should be about 200—300 words.

Unit 2

WAR AND CIVILIZATION

Never, never, never believe any war will be smooth and easy, or that anyone who embarks on the strange voyage can measure the tides and hurricanes he will encounter. The statesman who yields to war fever must realize that once the signal is given, he is no longer the master of policy but the slave of unforeseeable and uncontrollable events.

—By Sir Winston Churchill

Learning Objectives

Upon completion of this unit, you should be able to:

Remember & Understand	★ summarize the historical events and compare the personalities of the great leaders mentioned in this unit; ★ identify and explain in your own words the thesis and the major points of text A and text B;
Analyze & Apply	★ use root words to make new words; ★ make reference to the thesis and the major points of text A and text B in your writing; ★ produce long, complicated sentences with infinitive phrases;
Evaluate & Create	★ incorporate adjectives in descriptive paragraphs; ★ participate in a discussion on the effect of war; ★ deliver a clear and coherent oral presentation of your impression of Chairman Mao.

Part One   Lead-in

Section 1   Listening

Task 1   Filling in the Blanks

Directions: Please fill in the blanks with one or two words on the basis of what you have heard in the passage.

History is full of examples of leaders joining together to meet common goals. But ___1___ have two leaders worked together with such friendship and ___2___ as American President Franklin Roosevelt and British Prime Minister Winston Churchill. The two men had much in common. They both were born to ___3___ and were active in politics for many years. Both men loved the sea and the navy, history and nature.

Roosevelt and Churchill first met when they were ___4___ in World War One. But neither man remembered much about that meeting. However, as they worked together during the Second World War, they came to like and ___5___ each other.

Roosevelt and Churchill ___6___ more than one thousand seven hundred letters and messages during five and a half years. They met many times, at large national gatherings and in ___7___. But the closeness of their friendship might be seen best in a story told by one of Roosevelt's ___8___, Harry Hopkins.

Hopkins remembered how Churchill was visiting Roosevelt at the White House one day. Roosevelt went into Churchill's room in the morning to say hello. But the president was ___9___ to see Churchill coming from the washing room with no clothes at all.

Roosevelt immediately ___10___ to the British leader for seeing him naked. But Churchill reportedly said: "The prime minister of Great Britain has nothing to hide from the president of the United States." And then both men laughed.

Task 2   Group Discussion

Directions: Please discuss the following questions in pairs or groups based on what you have heard.

1. What did Roosevelt and Churchill have in common?
2. Do you know any other stories about Roosevelt or Churchill?
3. Please retell the story told by Harry Hopkins in your own words.

Section 2   Watching

Task 1   Group Discussion

Directions: Please watch the video "Pearl Harbor" and discuss the following questions in pairs or groups.

1. What historical event is the video clip about? What do you know about this historical event?
2. In your opinion, what's the purpose of calling the local dentist?
3. In the video clip, did the Americans agree with each other as to how to react to the intelligence they had intercepted? According to your knowledge, what's the significance of this event?

Task 2 Dubbing

Directions: Please watch the video again, and then try to dub the voice of the following characters in a group of three.

Captain Thurman:	Sir, I believe they'll try to hit us... where it'll hurt us the most—Pearl Harbor.
Admiral:	It's over 4,000 nautical miles from Japan to Pearl. That's a long distance to steam a navy, Captain. Your theory is based on what?
Captain Thurman:	Well, it's what I would do.
Admiral:	That's not exactly hard evidence, Captain Thurman.
Captain Thurman:	Well, Admiral, if I had hard evidence, we'd already be at war.
Vice Admiral:	Sir, we can read their diplomatic codes, faster than they can type them. But Captain Thurman's cryptology team is still trying to crack the naval codes.
Captain Thurman:	The intercepts have missing words and garbled lines, so to explain the decrypts, we have to try to interpret what we think they're trying to do.
Admiral:	Interpret? You mean guess.
Vice Admiral:	They use their informed intuition, sir.
Captain Thurman:	We guess. It's like playing chess in the dark. Any rumor, troop movement, ship movement, spine-tingle, goose bump, we pay attention to it. When I was in the Asiatic Fleet, the locals used to try to get outside of a problem to try to see the inside. Well, I see a strike on Pearl. It's the worst thing that could happen. A blow to Pearl would devastate the Pacific Fleet's ability to make war.
Admiral:	So, sir, you would have us mobilize the entire fleet at the cost of millions of dollars based on this spine-tingling feeling of yours?
Captain Thurman:	No, sir. I understand my job is to gather and interpret material. Making difficult decisions based on incomplete information from my limited decoding ability is your job, sir.
Admiral:	Then break the damn naval code, Captain, so I can make a better decision.
Captain Thurman:	Aye, sir. We are trying.

Part Two   Reading and Writing

Text A

Grant and Lee: A Study in Contrasts
Bruce Catton

When Ulysses S. Grant and Robert E. Lee met in the parlor of a modest house at Appomattox Court House, Virginia, on April 9, 1865, to work out the terms for the

surrender of Lee's Army of Northern Virginia, a great chapter in American life came to a close, and a great new chapter began. These men were bringing the Civil War to its *virtual* finish. And the little room where they wrote out the terms was the scene of one of the *poignant*, dramatic contrasts in American history.

2   They were two strong men, these oddly different generals, and they represented the strengths of two *conflicting* currents that, through them, had come into final *collision.*

3   Back of Robert E. Lee was the notion that the old noble concept might somehow *survive* and be *dominant* in American life.

4   Lee was tidewater(沿海低地)Virginia, and in his background were family, culture, and tradition ... the age of chivalry(骑士精神)transplanted to a New World which was making its own legends and its own myths. He *embodied* a way of life that had *come down* through the age of knighthood(骑士身份)and the English country squire(乡绅). America was a land that was beginning all over again, *dedicated* to nothing much more complicated than the rather hazy belief that all men had equal rights and should have an equal chance in the world. In such a land, Lee *stood for* the feeling that it was somehow of advantage to human society to have a noticeable inequality in the social structure. There should be a leisure class, backed by ownership of land; in turn, society itself should be *keyed to* the land as the chief source of wealth and influence. It would *bring forth* (according to this ideal) a class of men with a strong sense of *obligation* to the community; men who lived not to gain advantage for themselves, but to meet the solemn obligations which had been laid on them by the very fact that they were *privileged*. From them the country would get its leadership; to them it could look for the higher values—of thought, of conduct, of personal deportment（风度）—to give it strength and virtue.

5   Grant, the son of a tanner(制革工)on the Western frontier, was everything Lee was not. He had come up *the hard way* and embodied nothing in particular except the *eternal* toughness and strong fiber of the men who grew up beyond the mountains. He was one of a body of men who owed respect and admiration to no one, who were self-reliant *to a fault*, who cared hardly anything for the past but who had a sharp eye for the future.

6   These frontier men were the *precise* opposites of the tidewater aristocrats. Back of them, in the great *surge* that had taken people over the Alleghenies and into the opening Western country, there was a deep, *implicit* dissatisfaction with a past that had *settled into grooves*. They stood for democracy, not from any reasoned conclusion about the proper ordering of human society, but simply because they had grown up in the middle of democracy and knew how it worked. Their society might have privileges but they would be privileges each man had won for himself. Forms and patterns meant nothing. No man was born to anything, except perhaps to a chance to show how far he could rise. Life was competition.

7   Yet along with this feeling had come a deep sense of belonging to a nationa

community. The Westerner who developed a farm, opened a shop, or set up in business as a trader, could hope to *prosper* only as his own nation prospered. If the land was settled, with towns and highways and *accessible* markets, he could better himself. He saw his fate in terms of the nation's own *destiny*.

And that, perhaps, is where the contrast between Grant and Lee becomes most striking. The Virginia aristocrat, inevitably, saw himself in relation to his own region. He lived in a static society, which could endure almost anything except change. Instinctively, his first loyalty would go to the *locality* in which that society existed.

The Westerner, on the other hand, would fight with an equal tenacity(固执)for the broader concept of society. He fought so because what he lived by would survive or fall with the nation itself. He could not possibly *stand by* unmoved *in the face of* an attempt to destroy the Union. He would combat it with everything he had, because he could only see it as an effort to cut the ground out from under his feet.

So Grant and Lee were in complete contrast, representing two completely opposed elements in American life. Grant was the modern man emerging; beyond him, ready to come on the stage, was the great age of steel and machinery, of crowded cities and a restless burgeoning(迅速发展的)vitality. Lee might have ridden down from the old age of chivalry, lance in hand, silken banner *fluttering* over his head. Each man was the perfect champion of his cause, drawing both his strengths and weaknesses from the people he led.

Yet, it was not all contrast, after all. Different as they were—in background, in personality, in *underlying aspiration*—these two great soldiers had much in common. Under everything else, they were marvelous fighters. Furthermore, their fighting qualities were really very much alike.

Lastly, and perhaps greatest of all, there was the ability, at the end, to turn quickly from war to peace once the fighting was over. Out of the way these two men behaved at Appomattox came the possibility of a peace of *reconciliation*. Their behavior there put all succeeding generations of Americans in their debt. Two great Americans, Grant and Lee—very different, yet under everything very much alike. Their *encounter* at Appomattox was one of the great moments of American history.

(983 words)

surrender	[səˈrendə(r)]	v.	to stop fighting and admit defeat 投降
virtual	[ˈvɜːtʃʊəl]	a.	almost a particular thing or quality 几乎……的；实质上的
poignant	[ˈpɔɪnjənt]	a.	causing or having a very sharp feeling of sadness 令人痛苦的,酸楚的；深深打动人的

conflict	[ˈkɒnflɪkt]	n.	an active disagreement between people with opposing opinions or principles 冲突,分歧,争论
collision	[kəˈlɪʒ(ə)n]	n.	a strong disagreement 冲突,抵触
survive	[səˈvaɪv]	v.	to continue to live or exist, esp. after coming close to dying or being destroyed or after being in a difficult or threatening situation 继续生存,存活,(尤指)幸存
dominant	[ˈdɒmɪnənt]	a.	more important, strong or noticeable than anything else of the same type 主要的,主导的,占优势的
embody	[ɪmˈbɒdi]	v.	to represent a quality or an idea exactly 具体表现,体现
dedicate	[ˈdedɪkeɪt]	v.	to give your energy, time, etc. completely 奉献,献出(全部精力、时间等)
obligation	[ˌɒblɪˈɡeɪʃ(ə)n]	n.	a moral or legal duty to do sth. 义务,责任,职责
privileged	[ˈprɪv(ə)lɪdʒd]	a.	having a privilege 享有特权的;特许的
eternal	[ɪˈtɜːnəl]	a.	lasting forever or for a very long time 永远的,永恒的;长期的
precise	[prɪˈsaɪs]	a.	exact and accurate 精确的,准确的,确切的
surge	[sɜːdʒ]	n.	a sudden and great movement forward 涌现,奔涌
implicit	[ɪmˈplɪsɪt]	a.	suggested but not communicated directly 不明言的,含蓄的
prosper	[ˈprɒspə(r)]	a.	(of a person or a business) to be or become successful, esp. financially (人或企业)成功的;(尤指经济上)繁荣的,昌盛的
accessible	[əkˈsesəbl]	a.	able to be reached or easily got 可进入的,可接近的;可得到的
destiny	[ˈdestɪni]	n.	the things that will happen in the future 前途,命运
locality	[ləʊˈkæliti]	n.	a particular area 特定地区
flutter	[ˈflʌtə(r)]	v.	to make a series of quick delicate movements up and down or from side to side, or to cause sth. to do this (使)飘动,挥动,颤动;拍(翅),鼓(翼)
underlying	[ˌʌndəˈlaɪɪŋ]	a.	real but not immediately obvious 暗含的,深层的,潜在的
aspiration	[ˌæspɪˈreɪʃ(ə)n]	n.	sth. that you hope to achieve 志向,抱负,渴望达到的目标
reconciliation	[ˌrek(ə)nsɪliˈeɪʃ(ə)n]	n.	when two people or groups of people become friendly again after they have argued 和解,和好,修好
encounter	[ɪnˈkaʊntə(r)]	n.	a meeting, esp. one that happens by chance 偶然相遇,邂逅,不期而遇

Phrases and Expressions

come down	to have come from a long time in the past (从很久以前)流传下来
stand for	to support or represent a particular idea or set of ideas 支持,主张;代表

key ... to	to arrange or plan sth. so that it is suitable for a particular person or situation 使适合于；针对……安排（或计划）
bring forth	to cause sth. to happen or be seen or known 产生, 引起
the hard way	in the most difficult way, at a great cost 费力地, 艰难地
to a fault	used to say that sb. has a lot, or even too much, of a particular good quality（良好品质）过分, 过度
settle into grooves	stop developing 因循守旧
stand by	to allow sth. unpleasant to happen without doing anything to stop it 袖手旁观
in the face of	despite having to deal with a difficult situation or problem 不顾（困难等）

Notes

1. The text was excerpted and adapted from "Grant and Lee: A Study in Contrast," which was written as a chapter of *The American Story*, a collection of essays by noted historians. In this study, as in most of his other writings, Bruce Catton does more than recount the facts of history: he shows the significance within them. It is a carefully constructed essay, using contrast and comparison as the entire framework for his explanation.

2. The Author, Bruce Catton (1899—1978), was an American historian and journalist, best known for his books on the American Civil War. Known as a narrative historian, Catton specialized in popular history, featuring colorful characters and historical vignettes, in addition to the basic facts, dates, and analyses. Although his books were well researched and supported by footnotes, they were not generally presented in a rigorous academic style. He won a Pulitzer Prize in 1954 for *A Stillness at Appomattox* (1953), his study of the final campaign of the war in Virginia. He wrote many books, including *This Hallowed Ground* (1956), *Grant Moves South* (1960), *The Centennial History of the Civil War* (1961—1965), *Grant Takes Command* (1969), *Michigan: a Bicentennial History* (1976), *The Bold and Magnificent Dream: America's Founding Years, 1492—1815* (1978), *Reflections on the Civil War* (1982). For five years, Catton edited *American Heritage*.

Task 1 Generating the Outline

Directions: Please identify the thesis of the passage and the main point of each paragraph and find out how these points develop the thesis. You may use the table below to help you.

The thesis:	They were two strong men, these oddly different generals, and they represented the strengths of _____.
Part I [Paras. 1—2]: ***Introduction***	The Appomattox meeting brought the Civil War to its _____.

Part II [Paras. 3—10]: _____ between Grant and Lee	[Paras. 3—4] The type of American that _____; [Paras. 5—7] The type of American that _____. [Para. 8] Lee's concept of _____; [Para. 9] Grant's concept of _____. [Para. 10] Summary of _____: Grant & Lee
Part III [Paras. 11—12]: Despite their striking differences, they _____.	[Para. 11] Transitional paragraph from _____ to _____; [Para. 12] _____: Grant & Lee

Task 2 Understanding the Text

Directions: Please answer the following questions based on Text A.

1. Why did Catton mention the meeting at Appomatox in the introduction?
2. What are the major differences between the two men?
3. What similarities does Catton see between Grant and Lee?
4. What does "a great chapter in American life" and "a great new chapter" mean? (Para. 1)
5. What does each of them represent? (Para. 4 & Para. 5)
6. What does "a leisure class" refer to? (Para. 4)
7. What does Robert Lee indicate in this sentence: "There should be a leisure class, backed by ownership of land; in turn, society itself should be keyed to the land as the chief source of wealth and influence."? (Para. 4)
8. Why do these frontier men have such a deep dissatisfaction with the past? (Para. 6)
9. What does "it" in "he could only see it" refer to? What does "cut the ground out from under his feet" mean? (Para. 9)
10. What does "the great age of steel and machinery" refer to? (Para. 10)

Task 3 Vocabulary Building

Directions: Study the following five frequently used word roots and review the words you've learnt by adding prefixes or suffixes to the roots. One example is provided.

> domin[=dom]=house   priv=single, alone   dict, dic =say, assert
> spir = breathe   pet = seek

1. dom=house,表示"屋,家"

dome	n.	圆屋顶;大厦
domestic	a.	家里的;国内的(dom+estic 表形容词→家里的)
domesticate	v.	驯养(domestic 家里的+ate→使成为家里的→驯养动物)
dominate	v.	支配,统治(domin [=dom]+ate→像家长一样→统治)
indomitable	a.	不可征服的(in 不+ domitadle 可征服的)
predominant	a.	主要的,支配地位的(pre 在前面+dominant 支配的)

2. **priv=single, alone, 表示"单个"**
   private   a.   私人的(priv+ate→个人的)

3. **dict, dic=say, assert, 表示"说话,断言"**
   dictate   v.   口授;命令;听写(dict+ate 说话→口授;命令)

4. **spir=breathe, 表示"呼吸"**
   aspire   v.   热望;立志(a加强+spire→看到渴望的东西加强呼吸→热望)

5. **pet=seek, 表示"追寻,寻求"**
   petition   n.   请愿,申请(pet+ition→追寻状态→请愿)

Task 4 Learning the Phrases

Directions: Please fill in the blanks in the sentences below with the phrases listed in the box. Change the forms if necessary. Notice that some phrases need to be used more than once.

bring forth	come down	in particular	stand for
in the face of	stand by	to a fault	

1. Certain Wiccan mythology holds that Wicca has _____ from the Stone Age, surviving persecution in secret covens for hundreds of years.
2. During the war Dagestan, and _____ the Botlikh region, became a conduit for weapons and men into and out of Chechnya.
3. Tracing his political lineage to the New Deal and Great Society, he _____ higher spending on domestic programs.
4. Our fleets number thousands upon thousands of craft and we would not _____ and allow your precious Earth to be violated.
5. My wife is neat _____. If I drop a single ash on the rag, she comes running with the vacuum cleaner.
6. But a frontal attack _____ barbed wire and entrenched machine-guns was unlikely to succeed, and it guaranteed heavy losses.
7. I know many citizens have fears tonight, and I ask you to be calm and resolute, even _____ a continuing threat.
8. Even Greece, which _____ Serbia during the Balkan war and is considered its closest ally, has called on Milosevic to honor the November vote.
9. He still hoped that the Revolution would _____ some good result, but could not suppress his fears.
10. The Gulf crisis also contributed to a fall in revenue from tourism, which accounted for 9 percent of gross domestic product (GDP); UK and US visitors _____ brought less income.

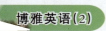

Task 5   Studying the Sentence Structure

Infinitive Phrases

Sentences from the text

1. It would bring forth (according to this ideal) a class of men with a strong sense of obligation to the community; men who lived not <u>to gain advantage for themselves</u>, but <u>to meet the solemn obligations which had been laid on them by the very fact that they were privileged</u>. (Para. 4)
2. He could not possibly stand by unmoved in the face of an attempt <u>to destroy the Union</u>. (Para. 9)

Directions: Please follow the examples and create two sentences on your own, using infinitive phrases.

Tips

1. We use the infinitive to express purpose.
2. We use the infinitive as a post modifier after abstract nouns like: *ability, desire, need, wish, attempt,* and so on.
3. We often use a to-infinitive as a post modifier after an indefinite pronoun.

1. _____
   _____

2. _____
   _____

Task 6   Paraphrasing Difficult Sentences

1. They were two strong men, these oddly different generals, and they represented the strengths of two conflicting currents that, through them, had come into final collision.
   _____

2. America was a land that was beginning all over again, dedicated to nothing much more complicated than the rather hazy belief that all men had equal rights and should have an equal chance in the world.
   _____
   _____

3. From them the country would get its leadership; to them it could look for the higher values—of thought, of conduct, of personal deportment—to give it strength and virtue.
   _____
   _____

4. Back of them, in the great surge that had taken people over the Alleghenies and into the opening Western country, there was a deep, implicit dissatisfaction with a past that had settled into grooves.
   _____
   _____

5. Grant was the modern man emerging; beyond him, ready to come on the stage, was the great age of steel and machinery, of crowded cities and a restless burgeoning vitality.

Task 7 Summarizing the Text

Directions: Please summarize Text A in 100 words. You may use the table in Task 1 to help you.

Task 8 Writing with Adjectives

Directions: Now write a passage of two paragraphs to describe a great general in the history. In the first paragraph, you should describe his appearance. In the second paragraph, you should introduce his personality and his achievements. Your writing should be about 200 words.

Tips

1. Adjectives can tell us how things look, feel, taste, sound, or smell. They also describe how you feel about something. In Text A, Bruce Catton uses his sentences and words effectively to describe the two generals. The essay is laden with imagery to paint a vivid picture for the readers. For example, "And the little room where they wrote out the terms was the scene of one of the <u>poignant</u>, <u>dramatic</u> contrasts in American history." "They were two <u>strong</u> men, these <u>oddly different</u> generals, and they represented the strengths of two <u>conflicting</u> currents that, through them, had come into final collision." "He had come up the hard way and embodied nothing in particular except the eternal toughness and <u>strong</u> fiber of the men who grew up beyond the mountains." "Beyond him, ready to come on the stage, was the <u>great</u> age of steel and machinery, of <u>crowded</u> cities and a <u>restless burgeoning</u> vitality."

2. You need to include colorful adjectives, such as adjectives of feature, quality, etc. in both paragraphs to make your writing more effective and picturesque.

Part Three　Reading and Speaking

Text B

Soviet Strong Man
Edgar Snow

1　　I met Mao soon after my arrival: a very thin, rather Lincolnesque(像林肯的)figure, above *average* height for a Chinese, somewhat *stooped*, with a head of thick black hair grown very long, and with large, searching eyes, a high bridged nose and *prominent* cheekbones. My *fleeting* impression was of an *intellectual* face of great shrewdness, but I had no opportunity to *verify* this for several days. Next time I saw him, Mao was walking hatless along the street at dusk, talking with two young peasants and gesturing earnestly. I did not recognize him until he was pointed out to me—moving along *unconcernedly* with the rest of the *strollers*, despite the $250,000 which Nanking had hung over his head.

2　　The influence of Mao Tse-tung throughout the Communist world of China was probably greater than that of anyone else. He was a member of nearly everything—the revolutionary military committee, the political bureau of Central Committee, the finance commission, the organization committee, the public health *commission,* and others. His real influence was *asserted* through his domination of the political bureau, which had decisive power in the policies of the Party, the government, and the army.

3　　Mao seemed to me a very interesting and complex man. He had the simplicity and naturalness of the Chinese peasant, with a lively sense of humor and a love of *rustic* laughter. His laughter was even active on the subject of himself and the shortcomings of the soviets—a boyish sort of laughter which never in the least shook his inner faith in his purpose. He was plain-speaking and plain-living, and some people might have considered him rather *coarse* and vulgar. Yet he combined curious qualities of naïveté with incisive(锐利的)wit and worldly sophistication.

4　　Mao was an *accomplished* scholar of Classical Chinese, an omnivorous(兴趣广泛的)reader, a deep student of philosophy and history, a good speaker, a man with an unusual memory and extraordinary powers of concentration, an able writer, careless in his personal habits and appearance but astonishingly meticulous about details of duty, a man of tireless energy, and a military and political strategist of considerable genius. It was interesting that many Japanese regarded him as the ablest Chinese strategist alive.

5　　Mao lived with his wife in a two-room yao-fang with bare, poor, map-covered walls. He had known much worse, and as the son of a "rich" peasant in Hunan he had also known better. The Mao's chief luxury (like Chou's) was a mosquito net. Otherwise Mao lived very much like *the rank and file* of the Red Army. After ten years of leadership of the Reds, after hundreds of confiscations(没收) of property of landlords, officials, and tax collectors, he owned only his blankets and a few personal belongings, including two cotton uniforms. Although he was a Red Army commander as well as chairman, he wore on his coat collar only the two red bars that are the badge of ordinary Red soldier.

Mao's food was the same as everybody's, but being a Hunanese he had the southerner's ai-la, or "love of pepper." He even had pepper cooked into his bread. Except for this passion, he scarcely seemed to notice what he ate. One night at dinner I heard him *expand on* a theory of pepper-loving peoples being revolutionaries. He first *submitted* his own province, Hunan, famous for the revolutionaries it has produced. Then he listed Spain, Mexico, Russia, and France to support his contention, but laughingly had to admit defeat when somebody mentioned the well-known Italian love of red pepper and garlic, in *refutation* of his theory.

I found him surprisingly well informed on current world politics. Mao was exceptionally well read in world history and had a realistic conception of European social and political conditions. His opinion of President Roosevelt was rather interesting. He believed him to be anti-Fascist, and thought China could cooperate with such a man. He asked *innumerable* questions about the New Deal, and Roosevelt's foreign policy. The questioning showed a remarkably clear conception of the objectives of both.

Mao was an ardent student of philosophy. Once when I was having nightly interviews with him on Communist history, a visitor brought him several new books on philosophy, and Mao asked me to postpone our *engagements*. He consumed those books in three or four nights of intensive reading, during which he seemed unaware of everything else. He had not confined his reading to Marxist philosophers, but also knew something of the ancient Greeks, of Spinoza, Kant, Goethe, Hegel, Rousseau, and others.

Mao worked thirteen or fourteen hours a day, often until very late at night, frequently *retiring* at two or three. He seemed to have an iron *constitution*. That he traced to a youth spent in hard work on his father's farm, and to an austere(艰苦的) period in his schooldays when he had formed a kind of Spartan(斯巴达式的) club with some comrades. They used to *fast*, go on long hikes in the wooded hills of South China, swim in the coldest weather, walk shirtless in the rain and sleet—to toughen themselves.

Mao impressed me as a man of considerable depth of feeling. I remember that his eyes moistened once or twice when he was speaking of dead comrades, or recalling incidents in his youth, during the rice riots and famines of Hunan, when some starving peasants were beheaded in his province for demanding food from the yamen. One soldier told me of seeing Mao give his coat away to a wounded man at the front. They said that he refused to wear shoes when the Red warriors had none.

11   Except for a few weeks when he was ill, he walked most of the 6,000 miles of the Long March, like the rank and file. He could have achieved high office and riches by "*betraying*" to Kuomintang, and this applied to most Red commanders. The tenacity with which these Communists for ten years *clung to* their principles could not be fully evaluated unless one knew the history of "silver bullets" in China, by means of which other *rebels* were *bought off*.

(1007 words)

average	[ˈæv(ə)rɪdʒ]	a.	typical and usual 普通的, 平常的, 中等的, 一般的
stooped	[stuːpt]	a.	standing or walking with your head and shoulders bent forwards 弓背站立(或行走)的
prominent	[ˈprɒmɪnənt]	a.	sticking out from a surface 凸出的
fleeting	[ˈfliːtɪŋ]	a.	short or quick 短暂的, 迅速的
intellectual	[ˌɪnt(ə)lˈektjʊəl]	n.	a very educated person whose interests are studying and other activities that involve careful thinking and mental effort 知识分子, 脑力劳动者
verify	[ˈverɪfaɪ]	v.	to prove that sth. exists or is true, or to make certain that sth. is correct 证明, 证实
unconcerned	[ˌʌnkənˈsɜːnd]	a.	not worried or not interested, esp. when you should be worried or interested (尤指应当担心或感兴趣时)不担心的, 漠不关心的, 无兴趣的
stroller	[ˈstrəʊlə(r)]	n.	someone who strolls 散步者, 闲逛者
commission	[kəˈmɪʃ(ə)n]	n.	a group of people who have been formally chosen to discover information about a problem or examine the reasons why the problem exists (负责调查问题真相或原因的)委员会
assert	[əˈsɜːt]	v.	to start to have an effect 生效, 起作用
rustic	[ˈrʌstɪk]	a.	simple and often rough in appearance; typical of the countryside 粗制的, 乡村的, 乡村特色的; 质朴的
coarse	[kɔː(r)s]	a.	rude and offensive 粗俗的, 粗野的, 无礼的
accomplished	[əˈkʌmplɪʃt]	a.	skilled 熟练的; 有造诣的, 有才艺的
submit	[səbˈmɪt]	v.	to suggest 建议, 主张
contention	[kənˈtenʃ(ə)n]	n.	an opinion expressed in an argument 论点; 主张, 看法

refutation	[ˌrefjʊˈteɪʃ(ə)n]	n.	the overthrowing of an argument, opinion, testimony, doctrine or theory by argument or countervailing proof 驳斥,反驳,否认……的正确性(或真实性)
innumerable	[ɪˈnjuːmərəbl]	a.	too many to be counted 无数的,数不清的
engagement	[ɪnˈɡeɪdʒmənt]	n.	an arrangement to meet someone or do sth. at a particular time 约定,约会,预约
retire	[rɪˈtaɪə(r)]	v.	to go to bed 就寝,上床睡觉
constitution	[ˌkɒnstɪˈtjuːʃ(ə)n]	n.	the general state of someone's health 体质,体格
fast	[fɑːst]	v.	to eat no food for a period of time 禁食,斋戒
betray	[bɪˈtreɪ]	v.	not to be loyal to your country or a person, often by doing sth. harmful such as helping their enemies 背叛,出卖,对……不忠诚
rebel	[ˈreb(ə)l]	n.	a person who fights against the government of their country 反政府的人;叛乱者,造反者

Phrases & Expressions

the rank and file	the ordinary soldiers who are not officers 普通士兵
expand on	to give more details about sth. you have said or written 对……详述,进一步说明
cling to	to refuse to stop believing or hoping for sth. 坚持,保持,死死抱住(信念或希望)
buy off	to pay someone so that they do not cause you any trouble 买通,贿赂(某人)

Notes

1. *Red Star Over China*, a 1937 book by Edgar Snow, is an account of the Communist Party of China written when they were a guerrilla army still obscure to Westerners. It was the most influential book on Western understanding and sympathy for China in the 1930s. In *Red Star Over China*, Edgar Snow recounts the months that he spent with the Chinese Red Army in 1936. Snow uses his extensive interviews with Mao and the other top leaders to present vivid descriptions of the Long March, as well as biographical accounts of the leaders.

2. Edgar Snow was an American journalist known for his books and articles on Communism in China and the Chinese Communist revolution. He went to the Far East when he was 22. He made his home in China for twelve years, studied the country and the language, and lectured at Yenching University. As a foreign correspondent in China, Burma, India, and Indochina he worked successively for the *Chicago Tribune, New York Sun, New York Herald Tribune*, and

London Daily Herald. Then, as associate editor of the *Saturday Evening Post*, he reported wartime and postwar events in Asia and Europe, and became its widely quoted specialist on China, India, and the U.S.S.R. He is the author of eleven books, including *The Battle for Asia, People on Our Side, Journey to the Beginning, Red China Today: The Other Side of the River*, and *The Long Revolution*. He died in 1972.

Task 1　Summarizing

Directions: Snow talked about his impression of Mao by elaborating on some striking characteristics of Mao. Please summarize these characteristics in your own words.

Task 2　Discussion

Directions: Throughout history, there have been numerous wars, which were bloody and devastating. But some wars had to be fought. Please work in groups and discuss the profound effects of war on the fate of a nation and the future of a country, taking the American Civil War and Chinese Anti-Japanese War as examples.

Task 3　Presentation

Directions: Mao Tse-tung is a household name, and everyone knows something about this great man. Is the image of this legendary man in your mind the same as that depicted in Snow's writings? In which aspects are they similar? In which aspects different? Give an oral presentation to talk about your impression of Chairman Mao.

Part Four　Cross Cultural Communication

Passage A

黄埔军校简史

黄埔军校是伟大的民主革命先行者孙中山先生创立的中国第一所新型军事干部学校,名为"陆军军官学校"。1924年6月16日军校在广州开学,因校址设在黄埔长洲岛,故通称"黄埔军校"。军校创办后,国共两党都选派重要干部到校任职。孙中山先生亲自兼任校总理,蒋介石任校长,廖仲恺任国民党党代表,中国共产党人周恩来、熊雄先后担任军校政治部主任。孙中山亲自批准将这样一幅对联贴在军校大门上:"升官发财行往他处,贪生畏死勿入斯门"。

军校以孙中山提出的"创造革命军,来挽救中国的危亡"为宗旨,以"亲爱精诚"为校训,采取军事与政治并重、理论与实践结合的教育方针,为国共两党培养、造就了大批军事政治人才。在国民党方面,黄埔师生被授予上将军衔的有近40人。在共产党方面,中国人民解放军十大元帅中有5人出自黄埔,10名大将中黄埔出身的占了3位、1955年授衔的57名上将中有黄埔师生9人。

黄埔军校在广州创办后,历经南京、成都时期,共开办了23期。黄埔军校作为第一次国共合作的历史见证,在中国现代史和军事史上都具有重要意义。国共两党的黄埔师生在平定商团叛乱和东征、北伐战争中,英勇顽强,不怕牺牲,所向披靡,立下了不朽的功勋。抗日战争爆发后,黄埔师生再度携手,并肩作战,无役不从,为民族解放战争的胜利作出了重要贡献。从东征、北伐到十年内战,从抗日到解放战争,黄埔师生都是这段战争史的主角。人类军事史上,很少有一个军校像黄埔军校那样,在如此短的时间内,那么深刻地影响了一个国家的历史。

(623字)

注解

1. 本文节选、改编自 http://news.xinhuanet.com/mil/2004-06/16/content_1529614.htm。
2. 作者陈斌华、陈键兴为新华社记者。

Word Bank

黄埔军校	Whampoa	先行者	forerunner
总理	premier	亲自	in person
校长	commandant	政治部主任	instructors in the political department
校训	motto	亲爱精诚	camaraderie
北伐	Northern Expedition	抗日战争	Anti-Japanese War

Directions: Please summarize the passage in English. Your summary should be about 150 — 200 words.

_____
_____
_____
_____
_____
_____
_____
_____

Passage B

A Brief History of West Point

West Point's role in [America's] history dates back to the Revolutionary War, when both sides realized the strategic importance of the commanding plateau on the west bank of the Hudson River. General George Washington considered West Point to be the most important strategic position in America. Washington personally selected Thaddeus Kosciuszko, one of the heroes of Saratoga, to design the fortifications for West Point in 1778, and Washington transferred his headquarters to West Point in 1779. Continental soldiers built forts, batteries and redoubts and extended a 150-ton iron chain across the Hudson to control river traffic. Fortress West Point was never captured by the British, despite Benedict Arnold's treason. West Point is the oldest continuously occupied military post in America.

Several soldiers and legislators, including Washington, Knox, Hamilton and John Adams, desiring to eliminate America's wartime reliance on foreign engineers and artillerists, urged the creation of an institution devoted to the arts and sciences of warfare.

President Thomas Jefferson signed legislation establishing the United States Military Academy in 1802. He took this action after ensuring that those attending the Academy would be representative of a democratic society.

Colonel Sylvanus Thayer, the "father of the Military Academy," served as Superintendent from 1817—1833. He upgraded academic standards, instilled military discipline and emphasized honorable conduct. Aware of our young nation's need for engineers, Thayer made civil engineering the foundation of the curriculum. For the first half century, USMA graduates were largely responsible for the construction of the bulk of the nation's initial railway lines, bridges, harbors and roads.

After gaining experience and national recognition during the Mexican and Indian wars, West Point graduates dominated the highest ranks on both sides during the Civil War. Academy graduates, headed by generals such as Grant, Lee, Sherman and Jackson, set high standards of military leadership for both the North and South.

The development of other technical schools in the post-Civil War period allowed West Point to broaden its curriculum beyond a strict civil engineering focus. Following the creation of Army post-graduate command and staff schools, the Military Academy came to be viewed as the first step in a continuing Army education.

In World War I, Academy graduates again distinguished themselves on the battlefield. After the war, Superintendent Douglas MacArthur sought to diversify the academic curriculum. In recognition of the intense physical demands of modern warfare, MacArthur pushed for major changes in the physical fitness and intramural athletic programs. "Every cadet an athlete" became an important goal. Additionally, the cadet management of the Honor System, long an unofficial tradition, was formalized with the creation of the Cadet Honor Committee.

Eisenhower, MacArthur, Bradley, Arnold, Clark, Patton, Stilwell and Wainwright were among an impressive array of Academy graduates who met the challenge of leadership in the Second World War. The postwar period again saw sweeping revisions to the West Point curriculum resulting from the dramatic developments in science and technology, the increasing need to understand other cultures and the rising level of general education in the Army.

In 1964, President Johnson signed legislation increasing the strength of the Corps of Cadets from 2,529 to 4,417 (more recently reduced to 4,000). To keep up with the growth of the Corps, a major expansion of facilities began shortly thereafter.

Another significant development at West Point came when enrollment was opened to women in 1976. Sixty-two women graduated in the class of 1980, to include Andrea Hollen, Rhodes Scholar. Just as women are a vital and integral part of the U.S. Army, so they are at West Point.

In recent decades, the Academy's curricular structure was markedly changed to permit cadets to major in any one of more than a dozen fields, including a wide range of subjects from the sciences to the humanities. From the day of its founding, West Point has grown in its size and stature, but it remains committed to the task of producing commissioned leaders of character for America's Army. Today, the Academy graduates more than 900 new officers annually, which represents approximately 20 percent of the new lieutenants required by the Army each year. The student body, or Corps of Cadets, numbers 4,400, of whom approximately 15 percent are women.

Ever mindful of its rich heritage, West Point continues to prepare its graduates to serve as commissioned leaders of character in America's 21st Century Army. Guided by its timeless motto, "Duty, Honor, Country," the Academy is poised confidently to provide the Army and the Nation with its third century of service.

(746 words)

Notes

The passage was retrieved and adapted from: http://www.usma.edu/wphistory/SitePages/Home.aspx.

Directions: Please summarize the passage in Chinese. Your summary should be about 200—300 words.

Unit 3

THE ROAD TO HAPPINESS

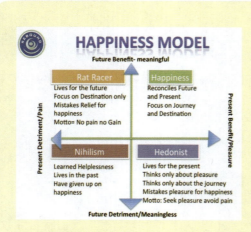

... with regard to what happiness is they differ, and the many do not give the same account as the wise. For the former think it is some plain and obvious thing, like pleasure, wealth, or honour; they differ, however, from one another and often even the same man identifies it with different things, with health when he is ill, with wealth when he is poor; but, conscious of their ignorance, they admire those who proclaim some great ideal that is above their comprehension. Now some thought that apart from these many goods there is another which is self-subsistent and causes the goodness of all these as well.

—From *Nicomachean Ethics* by Aristotle

Learning Objectives

Upon completion of this unit, you should be able to:

Remember & Understand	★ recognize the synonyms, antonyms and collocations related to happiness; ★ identify and explain in your own words the thesis and the major points of Text A and Text B;
Analyze & Apply	★ use root words to make new words; ★ make reference to the thesis and the major points of Text A and Text B in your writing; ★ recognize and produce adverbial clauses of reason;
Evaluate & Create	★ incorporate transitions in the description of a process; ★ synthesize information among related sources about philosophy of happiness and its applications in daily life; ★ deliver a clear and coherent oral presentation on your understanding of happiness.

Unit 3

Part One Lead-in

Section 1 Listening
Task 1   Filling in the Blanks

Directions: Please fill in the blanks with what you have heard in the passage.

Traits of Americans, 35-80 who report being very happy*

Good Health

24% of those in good health reported being very happy
vs
8% of those in poor health

Relationships

70% of those who are married or in a relationship are the happiest
vs
60% of singles

Children

72% said watching children or grandchildren succeed contributes to happiness

KISSES & HUGS
Kissing or hugging someone you love contributes a lot to happiness
71%

TRUSTWORTHY
Being told you are a person who can be trusted contributes a lot to happiness
71%

Income

28% of those with an income $125k+ report being very happy
vs
15% of those with an income under $25k

Income and happiness are positively correlated, but having money does not guarantee happiness. Increased income becomes a resource which can be applied to meaningful areas of one's life.

Pets

66% say spending time with a pet contributes a lot to happiness. That number is even higher for older females 65+ (81%) and singles (76%)

When Are People Happiest?
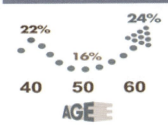
22% (40), 16% (50), 24% (60) AGE

Between ages 40 and 60, the early 50s are the lowest reported point of well-being. As people continue to age and eventually retire, they are able to devote more time to building relationships and enjoying simple everyday pleasures. By the early 60s, 24% of people report being *Very Happy*.

*Source: AARP Research Center, Beyond Happiness: Thriving, www.aarp.org
Design—Tony Clements / AARP

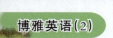

The Things that Make Americans Happy

In a recent study of Americans between the ages of 35 and 80, some questions were asked to get a better understanding of what brings happiness to the lives of individuals that are happy, ___1___. Many of the answers were pretty predictable, but there were a few surprises.

In the poll, 24% of Americans with ___2___ claimed to be happy, but only 8% in bad health ___3___. This is understandable due to the fact that we are often happiest when we are ___4___ by worry. So, staying healthy is the best way to ___5___.

It is clearly shown that the accomplishments of children and grandchildren lead to happiness. In the poll, 72% said that these accomplishments gave them ___6___. This type of pride found in these relationships is what many Americans ___7___.

Although health and family are often the most important factors linked to happiness, it has been established that ___8___. Only 15% of Americans making less than $25,000.00 a year claimed to be truly happy. This could be true for many different reasons, but a lack of income can lead to many problems that can hinder your ability to remain positive and content. Although money isn't everything, it is shown to ___9___ your happiness in some small way.

This study showed that individuals between the ages of 40 and 60 were often the most content. However, the 50's can sometimes be an adjustment period and can be difficult to navigate. As individuals in this age group ___10___, they often find their true happiness.

(http://www.aarp.org/content/dam/aarp/research/surveys_statistics/general/2013/infographics
Happiness-infographic-AARP-res-gen.pdf

Task 2 Group Discussion

Directions: Please discuss the following questions in pairs or groups based on what you have heard.

1. According to the passage you have just heard, what are the things that make the Americans happy To what extent do you agree or disagree with this opinion?

2. In the factors that lead to happiness, which one is the most important? Please use some evidence or data in the poll to support your point.

3. What are other factors contributing to your happiness as college students besides what you have heard from the passage?

Section 2 Watching

Directions: Before you watch, get familiar with the following new words and expressions.

triple [ˈtrɪp(ə)l]	n.	a quantity that is three times as great as another 三倍数
coincidentally [kəʊˌɪnsɪˈdentli]	ad.	happening at the same time 巧合地
flat-line [ˈflætˌlaɪn]	v.	to remain unchanged 持平
grand [grænd]	n	a thousand dollars or a thousand pounds 一千美元或英磅
extraneous [ɪkˈstreɪnɪəs; ek-]	a.	not relevant or essential to the situation you are involved in 无关的；不必要的

Unit 3

artery [ˈɑːtəri] (pl. arteries)	n.	the tubes in your body that carry blood from your heart to the rest of your body 动脉
stem [stem]	v.	to stop it spreading, increasing, or continuing 阻止
inflow [ˈɪnfləʊ]	n.	the process of flowing in 流入
mantra [ˈmæntrə]	n.	a statement or a principle that people repeat very often because they think it is true 准则
efficiency [ɪˈfɪʃ(ə)nsi]	n.	skillfulness in avoiding wasted time and effort 效率
rig up		to erect or construct, esp. as a temporary measure 临时搭建（尤指作为措施）
transformer furniture		变形金刚式的家具
fold away		to be capable of being folded up and stored 折叠
pop out of		to release sth. from sth. else so that it jumps or bursts out, possibly with a popping sound 蹦出
fold-down guest bed		可折叠式的客床

 Notes

1. The philosophy of Graham Hill is less stuff and happier life. He evangelizes the idea that living a pared-down life can make you happier, healthier and wealthier. And that editing down all the unnecessary and gratuitous stuff in your life will give you a smaller carbon footprint and a cleaner conscience.
2. Graham Hill is an entrepreneur, designer and environmentalist, the founder of TreeHugger.com and LifeEdited. He travels the world to tell stories of sustainability and minimalism.

(http://www.ted.com/talks/graham_hill_less_stuff_more_happiness)

Task 1 Group Discussion

Directions: Please watch the video "Less stuff, more happiness: the philosophy of Graham Hill" and discuss the following questions in pairs or groups.

1. What are the consequences of Americans' increasing consumption of goods in the past 50 years?
2. What are the benefits of possessing less stuff according to the speaker? And what evidence did he offer to develop his philosophy of less stuff and more happiness?
3. To what extent do you agree or disagree with his philosophy?

Task 2 Summary

Directions: Please watch the video again, and sum up the three main approaches the speaker suggested to apply his philosophy of less stuff and more happiness. Try to use appropriate transitions and adverbial clauses of reason in this process paragraph.

Graham Hill suggested <u>three</u> main approaches to apply his philosophy of less stuff and more happiness. First of all, _____.

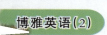

Secondly, _____.

Finally, _____.

Part Two   Reading and Writing

Text A

On Happiness
Aristotle

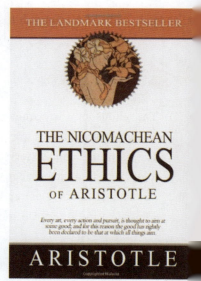

1   Now that we have spoken of the *virtues*, the forms of friendship, and the varieties of pleasure, what remains is to discuss in outline the nature of happiness, since this is what we state the *end* of human nature to be. Our discussion will be the more concise if we first sum up what we have said already. We said, then, that it is not a *disposition*; for if it were it might belong to some one who was asleep throughout his life, living the life of a plant, or, again, to some one who was suffering the greatest misfortunes. If these implications are unacceptable, and we must rather class happiness as an activity, as we have said before, and if some activities are necessary, and desirable for the sake of something else, while others are so in themselves, evidently happiness must be placed among those desirable in themselves, not among those desirable for the sake of something else; for happiness does not lack anything, but is self-*sufficient*. Now those activities are desirable in themselves from which nothing is sought beyond the activity. And of this nature *virtuous* actions are thought to be; for to do noble and good deeds is a thing desirable for its own sake.

2   Pleasant amusements also are thought to be of this nature; we choose them no for the sake of other things; for we are injured rather than benefited by them, since w are led to neglect our bodies and our property. But most of the people who are *deeme* happy *take refuge in* such *pastimes*, which is the reason why those who are *ready-witted* them are highly *esteemed* at the courts of tyrants; they make themselves pleasar companions in the tyrants' favourite *pursuits*, and that is the sort of man they wan Now these things are thought to be of the nature of happiness because people i despotic (专制的) positions spend their leisure in them, but perhaps such people pro nothing; for virtue and reason, from which good activities flow, do not depend c

despotic position; nor, if these people, who have never tasted pure and generous pleasure, take refuge in the bodily pleasures, should these for that reason be thought more desirable; for boys, too, think the things that are valued among themselves are the best. It is to be expected, then, that, as different things seem valuable to boys and to men, so they should to bad men and to good. Now, as we have often maintained, those things are both valuable and pleasant which are such to the good man; and to each man the activity *in accordance with* his own disposition is most desirable, and, therefore, to the good man that which is in accordance with virtue. Happiness, therefore, does not lie in amusement; it would, indeed, be strange if the end were amusement, and one were to take trouble and suffer hardship all one's life in order to amuse oneself. For, in a word, everything that we choose we choose for the sake of something else—except happiness, which is an end. Now to *exert* oneself and work for the sake of amusement seems silly and utterly childish. But to amuse oneself in order that one may exert oneself; for amusement is a sort of relaxation, and we need relaxation because we cannot work continuously. Relaxation, then, is not an end; for it is taken for the sake of activity.

The happy life is thought to be virtuous; now a virtuous life requires *exertion*, and does not consist in amusement. And we say that serious things are better than laughable things and those connected with amusement, and that the activity of the better of any two things—whether it be two elements of our being or two men—is the more serious; but the activity of the better is *superior* and more of the nature of happiness.

If happiness is activity in accordance with virtue, it is reasonable that it should be in accordance with the highest virtue; and this will be that of the best thing in us… That activity is *contemplative*. For, firstly, this activity is the best (since not only is reason the best thing in us, but the objects of reason are the best of knowable objects); and secondly, it is the most continuous, since we can *contemplate* truth more continuously than we can do anything. And we think happiness has pleasure *mingled with* it, but the activity of philosophic wisdom is admittedly the pleasantest of virtuous activities; *at all events* the pursuit of it is thought to offer pleasures marvellous for their purity and their enduringness, and it is to be expected that those who know will pass their time more pleasantly than those who inquire. And the self-sufficiency that is spoken of must belong most to the contemplative activity. For while a philosopher, as well as a just man or one possessing any other virtue, needs the necessaries of life, when they *are* sufficiently *equipped with* things of that sort the just man needs people towards whom and with whom he shall act justly, and the *temperate* man, the brave man, and each of the others is in the same case, but the philosopher, even when by himself, can contemplate truth, and the better the wiser he is; he can perhaps do so better if he has fellow-workers, but still he is the most self-sufficient. And this activity alone would seem to be loved for its own sake; for nothing *arises* from it apart from the contemplating, while from practical activities we gain more or less apart from the action. And happiness is thought to depend on leisure; for we are busy that we may have leisure, and make war that we may live in peace.

...

(989 words)

New Words

virtue	[ˈvɜːtjuː]	n.	the quality of doing what is right and avoiding what is wrong 美德
end	[end]	n.	goal 目标
disposition	[dɪspəˈzɪʃ(ə)n]	n.	your usual mood[心理] 性情；[syn.] temperament
sufficient	[səˈfɪʃ(ə)nt]	a.	of a quantity that can fulfill a need or requirement but without being abundant 足够的，充分的
virtuous	[ˈvɜːtjʊəs]	a.	morally excellent 善良的，有道德的
pastime	[ˈpɑːstaɪm]	n.	sth. that one does in his spare time pleasantly 娱乐，消遣
esteemed	[ɪsˈtiːmd]	a.	respected 受人尊敬的
deem	[diːm]	v.	to keep in mind or convey as a conviction or view 认为，视作，相信
ready-witted	[ˈredɪ ˈwɪtɪd]	a.	quick to learn or perceive 机敏的
pursuit	[pəˈsjuːt]	n.	the act of pursuing in an effort to overtake or capture 追赶，追求；[phrase] in pursuit of 寻求，追求；in hot pursuit 穷追不舍
exert	[ɪɡˈzɜːt]	v.	to make a great effort at a mental or physical task 运用，发挥；[phrase] exert oneself 尽力；exert an influence on 对……产生影响
exertion	[ɪɡˈzɜːʃn]	n.	use of physical or mental energy; hard work 发挥，运用；努力
superior	[suːˈpɪərɪə]	a.	上级的；优秀的，出众的；高傲的
contemplative	[kənˈtemplətɪv]	a.	thinking in a serious and calm way 沉思的
contemplate	[ˈkɒntempleɪt]	v.	to think intently and at length, as for spiritual purposes 沉思，思忖
temperate	[ˈtemp(ə)rət]	a.	not extreme in behavior 温和的；有节制的
arise	[əˈraɪz]	v.	to come into existence 出现；[phrase] arise from 由……引起，起因于

Unit 3

Phrases and Expressions

take refuge in	to appeal to sb. for sth., take shelter in 避难，求助于
in accordance with	in line with, in conformity to 依照；与……一致
be mingled with	to be mixed with 混杂
at all events	anyway, however, at all risks 无论如何
be equipped with	to be provided with, be armed with 配备有……，装有……

1. The text was an abridged excerpt from Book X, Chapter 6—7, *Nicomachean Ethics* by Aristotle（古希腊哲学家亚里士多德的著作《尼各马克伦理学》）translated by W. D. Ross. ***Nicomachean Ethics*** [nɪˌkɒmæˈkiːən; ˈeθɪks] is the name normally given to Aristotle's best-known work on ethics. The theme of the work is the Socratic question which had previously been explored in Plato's works, of how men should best live. Ethics, by Aristotle, is practical rather than theoretical. It is not only a contemplation about good living, but also aims to create good living. ***Nicomachean Ethics*** is widely considered one of the most important historical philosophical works, and had an important impact upon the European Middle Ages, becoming one of the core works of medieval philosophy. It therefore indirectly became critical in the development of all modern philosophy as well as European law and theology.

2. The author of the book, Aristotle ([ˈærɪˌstɒtəl]; 384 BC—322 BC), was a Greek philosopher and scientist born in the town of Stagira. At 18, he joined Plato's Academy in Athens and remained there until the age of 37 (c. 347 BC). His writings cover many subjects—including physics, biology, zoology, metaphysics, logic, ethics, aesthetics, poetry, theater, music, rhetoric, linguistics, politics and government—and constitute the first comprehensive system of Western philosophy. Shortly after Plato died, Aristotle left Athens and tutored Alexander the Great starting from 343 BC.

Task 1 Generating the Outline

Directions: Please identify the thesis of the passage and the main point of each paragraph and find out how these points develop the thesis. You may use the table below to help you.

The thesis:	To discuss in outline _____, since this is _____ _____.
Para. 1: Statement 1 and its reasons:	The nature of happiness is not _____, but a good activity.

Para. 2: **Statement 2 and its reasons:**	The nature of happiness is not _____, but a good activity.
Para. 3: **Statement 3 and its reasons:**	Happiness does not lie in amusements, but in _____, and a virtuous life requires _____.
Para. 4: **The best solution to happiness and its reasons:**	Happiness, which is activity _____ the highest virtue, is the _____ life. The reasons are as follows. Firstly, this activity is _____; secondly, this activity is the most _____; thirdly, happiness has _____ it, but the activity of philosophic wisdom is _____; and fourthly, the _____ must belong to the contemplative activity.

Task 2 Understanding the Text

Directions: Please answer the following questions based on Text A.

1. What issues have been touched upon before Aristotle comes to the discussion of the nature of happiness? (Para.1)
2. What, according to Aristotle, is the end of human nature? And what is the meaning of the word "end" in the text? (Para.1)
3. How does Aristotle prove his claim that the nature of happiness is not a disposition? (Para.1)
4. How does Aristotle define happiness? (Para.1)
5. Why, according to Aristotle, does happiness not lie in amusement, though people in despotic positions spend their leisure in them? (Para. 2)
6. Is it the end of human nature to exert oneself and work for the sake of amusement? (Para. 2)
7. Is relaxation an end of human nature? And why do we need relaxation? (Para. 2)
8. What does Aristotle claim to be the highest human activity or the highest pursuit in life? (Para. 4)
9. Could you figure out which part is possibly omitted in Para. 4, based on the structure of the first paragraph? And try to make it up. (Para. 4)
10. How much do you know about Aristotelian logic?

Task 3 Vocabulary Building

Directions: Study the following five frequently used word roots and review the words you have learnt by adding prefixes or suffixes to the roots. One example is provided.

> –pos–/–posit– =put;　　temper–/tempor– =time;　　–card–/– cord– =heart
> –ior =表形容词,"较……的";　　super– =表示"超级,超过,过度;在……上面"

1. -pos-, -posit- =put, 表示"放"

apposite	a.	适当的,得体的(ap加强动作+posite→放到(合适的位置)→适当的)
apposition	n.	并置,同位(ap+posit+ion→放在[一起]→并置)
compose	v.	组成;作曲;使镇定(com一起+pose→放到一起→组成)
composure	n.	镇静,沉着(com一起+pos+ure→[精神]放到一起→镇静)

Unit 3

composite	n.	合成物(com一起+posite→放到一起→合成物)
composition	n.	作文;组合(com一起+posit+ion→放到一起→组合→作文)
depose	v.	免职;沉淀(de去掉+pose放,职位→去掉职位→免职;de下去+pose→放下去→沉淀)
deposition	n.	免职;沉淀
deposit	v.	储存; n. 矿藏(de下面+posit→放下不用→储存)
disposition	n.	性情;安排(dis分开+posit+ion→分开放→安排;引申为人的喜好,心情)
discompose	v.	使不安(dis不+compose不镇静→使不安)
dispose	v.	处理;排列(dis分开→pose→分开[排好]→排列)
disposed	a.	愿意的(听任处理→心甘情愿的)
expose	v.	暴露;揭露(ex出+pose→放出来→暴露)
exposition	n.	展览;解释
indisposed	a.	不愿意的(in不+disposed情愿的)
impose	v.	强加;征税(im进+pose→放进去→强加)
imposition	n.	征税;强加
opposite	a.	相对的(op对+pos+ite→放到对面→相对的)
pose	v./n.	做姿态;姿态
proposal	n.	建议,提议(pro向前+pos+al→向前放→提建议)
purpose	n.	目的,意图(pur始终+pose→始终放的东西→目的)
posit	v.	本身是一个单词,意为"认为,肯定"
position	n.	立场(posit+ion→放出的[立场])
positive	a.	肯定的;积极的(posit肯定+ive)
repose	n.	休息,睡眠(re再+pose→再放下[工作]→休息)
transpose	v.	互换位置(trans转移+pose→[互相]移放)
supposition	n.	推测,猜想(sup在下面+posit+ion→放在下面的[想法]→推测)

2. temper-, /tempor- =time,表示"时间"或时间引起的现象

temporary	a.	临时的(tempor+ary→有时间性的→临时的)

3. -card-/-cord- =heart,表示"心脏;一致"

cardiac	a.	心脏的

4. -ior 表形容词,"较……的"

anterior	a.	较早的(anter早)

5. super-

① 表示"超级;超过,过度"

supersized	a.	超大型的(super+sized有范围的)

② 表示"在……上面"

supervise	v.	监视(super+vise看→在上面看→监视)

Task 4 Learning the Phrases

Directions: Please fill in the blanks in the sentences below with the phrases listed in the box. Change the forms if necessary. Notice that some phrases need to be used more than once.

| virtue and reason | exert oneself | arise from | in accordance with |
| be superior to | take refuge in | in the pursuit of | be mingled with |

1. Many great men have _____ humble beginnings.
2. If one does not _____ in youth, one will regret it in old age.
3. Humans have long enjoyed crowing about their intellectual _____ in the animal kingdom.
4. This abuse of authority _____ wealth is one of the dark sides of that developing country's economic miracle.
5. Business opportunity and education are the vehicles that people most often turn to _____ happiness.
6. The book _____ in *Plato and Aristotle* discusses the views of Plato and Aristotle in four related areas: eudaimonia, or living and acting well, as the ultimate end of action; virtues of character in relation to the emotions, and to one another; practical reasoning, especially from an end to ways or means; or action that is contrary to the agent's own judgment of what is best.
7. All concerned should act with a sense of care and responsibility, and _____ international law.
8. The human mind will always _____ machines because machines are only tools of human minds.
9. To live according to your pleasure, to go where you will, to stay where you will; in the spring to repose amid purple beds of flowers, in the autumn amid heaps of fallen leaves; to cheat the winter by basking in the sun and the summer by _____ cool shades, and to feel the force of neither unless it is your choice!
10. We long to _____ fresh green *Leaves of Grass* _____ these drier pages, to add Whitman's exhilarating justification of sense joy to Aristotle's exaltation of a purely intellectual happiness.

Task 5 Studying the Sentence Structure

Adverbial clauses of reason (ACOR)

Sentences from the text

1. <u>Now that</u> we have spoken of the virtues, the forms of friendship, and the varieties of pleasure, what remains is to discuss in outline the nature of happiness, <u>since</u> this is what we state the end of human nature to be. (Para. 1)
2. ...evidently happiness must be placed among those desirable in themselves, not among those desirable for the sake of something else; <u>for</u> happiness does not lack anything, but is self-sufficient. (Para. 1)
3. But most of the people who are deemed happy take refuge in such pastimes, which <u>is the reason why</u> those who are ready-witted at them are highly esteemed at the courts of tyrants; they make

themselves pleasant companions in the tyrants' favourite pursuits, and that is the sort of man they want. (Para. 2)

Directions: Text A contains many types of adverbial clauses of reason. Please sum up the typical sentence patterns of adverbial clauses of reason and then try to find out some examples.

The Usage of Adverbial Clauses of Reason

Adverbial Clause of Reason or Cause indicates why the particular action of the verb is taken. Fill in the table below to review the most commonly used types of adverbial clauses of reason.

Types of ACOR	English Transition Words, Phrases, and Sentences
Introduced by the subordinating conjunctions	*because, as, since, for, seeing (that), now (that)*
Introduced by the subordinating prepositional phrases	*because of, thank to, due to*
Introduced by clauses	*the reason why...is because...*
Introduced by infinitive verbs, expressing feelings and emotions	*(be) glad, happy, sorry, sad, worried, pleased, satisfied*
Introduced by gerunds	Clauses of reason which begin with the words *because, since,* and *as* omit such words in the adverb phrase. There are certain steps you must follow: • You must have the same subject in both clauses. • Delete the subject from the adverb clause. • Change the verb to -ing. • Delete the words *because, since* and *as*.

More examples from Text A

1. _____

2. _____

3. _____

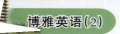

Task 6 Paraphrasing Difficult Sentences

1. Now that we have spoken of the virtues, the forms of friendship, and the varieties of pleasure, what remains is to discuss in outline the nature of happiness, since this is what we state the end of human nature to be.

2. Pleasant amusements also are thought to be of this nature; we choose them not for the sake of other things; for we are injured rather than benefited by them, since we are led to neglect our bodies and our property.

3. And we say that serious things are better than laughable things and those connected with amusement, and that the activity of the better of any two things—whether it be two elements of our being or two men—is the more serious; but the activity of the better is superior and more of the nature of happiness.

4. If happiness is activity in accordance with virtue, it is reasonable that it should be in accordance with the highest virtue; and this will be that of the best thing in us.

5. For while a philosopher, as well as a just man or one possessing any other virtue, needs the necessaries of life, when they are sufficiently equipped with things of that sort the just man needs people towards whom and with whom he shall act justly, and the temperate man, the brave man, and each of the others is in the same case, but the philosopher, even when by himself, can contemplate truth, and the better the wiser he is; he can perhaps do so better if he has fellow-workers, but still he is the most self-sufficient.

Task 7 Summarizing the Text

Directions: Please summarize Text A in 100—150 words. You may use the table in Task 1 to help you.

Task 8　Writing with Transitions

Directions: Summarize the reasons Aristotle provided to justify the claim that contemplative activity is the highest virtue. Try to use the adverbial clauses of reason and also connect the evidence and reasons with transitions of a process description. Your writing should be within 150 words.

Tips:

The description of a process should follow certain rules

- First of all, each paragraph in the body of a description of a process highlights a major stage of the procedure.
- Each stage may group several steps dependent upon the nature and complexity of the process being described.
- Specific steps are presented in chronological order. Definitions of specific terms and advice may be given by the author. No step can be left out as every step must be included!
- Transitional words and phrases are necessary so that each step and each paragraph lead logically to the next. Transitional words should not be repeated so often that they become tiring to the reader. A variety of transitional words should be used to keep your description of a process fresh and free flowing for the reader.

(http://www.michigan-proficiency-exams.com/description-of-a-process.html)

In the paragraph below, the transitional words are highlighted to give you a feel of how it's done.

Answering a question on WikiAnswers is easy! <u>First</u>, you sign onto the website using your identification and password. <u>Then</u>, look up a question using the "Ask" bar—or you can just browse the categories and see which questions you like! Click on the "Answer Question" button below the question and type your answer into the blank box. You can spell check your answer, too! <u>Then</u>, click the "Save" button and you have answered a question.

Part Three Reading and Speaking

Text B

Hamburger Model of Happiness
Tal Ben-Shahar

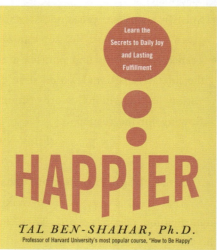

1   I was sixteen years old when I won the Israeli national *squash championship*. It was an event that brought the subject of happiness into sharp focus in my life.

2   I had always believed that winning the title would make me happy, would *alleviate* the emptiness I felt so much of the time. After all, it seemed clear to me that the mental and physical exertion were necessary to win the championship. Winning the championship was necessary for fulfillment. Fulfillment was necessary for happiness. That was *the logic* I operated *under*.

3   And, in fact, when I won the Israeli Nationals, I was *ecstatic*, happier than I had ever imagined myself being. But, after the night of celebration, the *tears* of joy *shed* only hours earlier turned to tears of pain and helplessness. For if I was not happy now, when everything seemed to have worked out perfectly, what *prospects* did I have of *attaining* lasting happiness?

4   I realized that I needed to think about happiness in different ways, to deepen or change my understanding of the nature of happiness. I *became obsessed with* the answer to a single question: how can I find lasting happiness? I pursued it *fervently*—I observed people who seemed happy and asked what it was that made them happy; I read everything I could find on the topic of happiness, from Aristotle to Confucius, from ancient philosophy to modern psychology, from academic research to self-help books.

5   ... Then I came up with the happiness model, *otherwise* known as the hamburger model. I thought of four kinds of hamburgers, each representing a *distinct archetype*, with each archetype describing a distinct pattern of attitudes and behaviors.

6   The first archetypal hamburger is the tasty junk-food burger. Eating this hamburger would *yield* present benefit, in that I would enjoy it, and future *detriment*, in that I would subsequently not feel well.

7   The experience of present benefit and future detriment defines the *hedonism*

archetype. Hedonists live by the *maxim* "Seek pleasure and avoid pain"; they focus on enjoying the present while ignoring the potential negative consequences of their actions.

The second hamburger type that came to mind was a tasteless vegetarian burger made with only the most healthful ingredients, which would afford me future benefit, in that I would subsequently feel good and healthy, and present detriment, in that I would not enjoy eating it.

The *corresponding* archetype is that of the rat race. The rat racer, subordinating the present to the future, suffers now for the purpose of some anticipated gain.

The third hamburger type, the worst of all possible burgers, is both tasteless and unhealthful: eating it, I would experience present detriment, in that it tastes bad, and suffer future detriment, in that it is unhealthful.

The parallel to this burger is the *nihilism* archetype. This archetype describes the person who has lost the lust for life; someone who neither enjoys the moment nor has a sense of future purpose.

The three archetypes that I came up with did not exhaust all possibilities—there was one more to consider. What about a hamburger that would be as tasty as the one I had turned down and as healthy as the vegetarian burger? A burger that would *constitute* a complete experience with both present and future benefit?

This hamburger exemplifies the happiness archetype. Happy people live *secure in the knowledge that* the activities that bring them enjoyment in the present will also lead to a fulfilling future.

The graph below illustrates the relationship between present and future benefit on the four archetypes. The *vertical axis* represents the future dimension of the experience, with future benefit on the top and future detriment on the bottom. The *horizontal* axis of the graph represents the present dimension of the experience, with present benefit on the right and present detriment on the left.

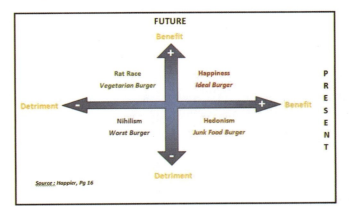

15 To varying degrees, and in different combinations, we all have characteristics of the rat racer, the hedonist, the nihilist, and the one who is happy.

16 The rat racer, the hedonist, and the nihilist are all, in their own ways, guilty of a *fallacy*—an inaccurate reading of reality, of the true nature of happiness and what it takes to lead a fulfilling life. The rat racer suffers from the "arrival fallacy"—the false belief that reaching a valued destination can *sustain* happiness. The hedonist suffers from the "floating moment fallacy"—the false belief that happiness can be sustained by an ongoing experience of momentary pleasures that *are detached from* a future purpose. Nihilism is also a fallacy, a misreading of reality—the false belief that no matter what one does, one cannot attain happiness. This last fallacy stems from the inability to see a synthesis between arrivals and floating moments, some third option that may provide a way out of one's unhappy *predicament*.

17 The rat racer's illusion is that reaching some future destination will bring him lasting happiness; he does not recognize the significance of the journey. The hedonist's illusion is that only the journey is important. The nihilist, having given up on both the destination and the journey, is *disillusioned* with life. The rat racer becomes a slave to the future; the hedonist, a slave to the moment; the nihilist, a slave to the past.

18 Attaining lasting happiness requires that we enjoy the journey on our way toward a destination we deem valuable. Happiness is not about making it to the peak of the mountain nor is it about climbing aimlessly around the mountain; happiness is the experience of climbing toward the peak.

(923 words)

New Words

squash	[skwɒʃ]	n.	a game played in an enclosed court by two or four players who strike the ball with long-handled rackets 壁球
championship	[ˈtʃæmpiənʃɪp]	n.	a competition to find the best player or team in a particular sport 锦标赛
alleviate	[əˈliːvɪeɪt]	v.	to provide physical relief, as from pain 减轻,缓和
ecstatic	[ɪkˈstætɪk]	a.	feeling very happy and full of excitement 欣喜若狂的
shed	[ʃed]	v.	to pour out in drops or small quantities or as if in drops or small quantities 流出
prospect	[ˈprɒspekt]	n.	the possibility of future success 前景
attain	[əˈteɪn]	v.	to gain with effort 获得,达到
fervently	[ˈfɜːvəntli]	ad.	enthusiastically, heart and hand 热心地,热诚地
otherwise	[ˈʌðəwaɪz]	ad.	in another and different manner 另外

Unit 3

distinct	[dɪˈstɪŋ(k)t]	a.	easy to perceive, esp. clearly outlined 独特的
archetype	[ˈɑːkɪtaɪp]	n.	an original model on which sth. is patterned 原型
yield	[jiːld]	v.	to give or supply 产生
detriment	[ˈdetrɪm(ə)nt]	n.	a damage or loss 损害
hedonism	[ˈhiːd(ə)nɪz(ə)m]	n.	the belief that gaining pleasure is the most important thing in life 享乐主义
maxim	[ˈmæksɪm]	n.	a rule for good or sensible behaviour, esp. one in the form of a saying 格言
corresponding	[ˌkɒrɪˈspɒndɪŋ]	a.	conforming in every respect 相应的
nihilism	[ˈnaɪ(h)ɪlɪz(ə)m]	n.	a belief which rejects all political and religious authority and current ideas in favour of the individual 虚无主义
constitute	[ˈkɒnstɪtjuːt]	v.	to form or compose 组成
vertical	[ˈvɜːtɪk(ə)l]	a.	standing or pointing straight up 垂直的
axis	[ˈæksɪs]	n.	the center around which sth. rotates 轴
horizontal	[hɒrɪˈzɒnt(ə)l]	a.	flat and level with the ground, rather than at an angle to it 地平线的
fallacy	[ˈfæləsɪ]	n.	a misconception resulting from incorrect reasoning 谬论
sustain	[səˈsteɪn]	v.	to continue it or maintain it for a period of time 保持
predicament	[prɪˈdɪkəm(ə)nt]	n.	an unpleasant situation that is difficult to get out of 困境
disillusion	[ˌdɪsɪˈl(j)uːʒ(ə)n]	v.	to free from enchantment 使醒悟,使不再抱幻想

Phrases & Expressions

under the logic	according to the logic 根据逻辑
shed tears	to pipe one's eye, weep 流泪
become obsessed with	to have or show excessive or compulsive concern with sth., be crazy about 着迷于
secure in the knowledge that	not worried because you are sure that nothing bad will happen 心里觉得踏实
be detached from	to be isolated from 与……隔绝

Notes

1. This passage was an abridged excerpt from *Happier: Learn the Secrets to Daily Joy & Lasting Fulfillment* (《幸福的方法》), published by McGraw Hill in 2007.
2. The author Tal Ben-Shahar (1970—   ), is an American and Israeli teacher, and writer in the areas of positive psychology and leadership. As a lecturer at Harvard University, Ben-Shahar created "Positive Psychology 1504," a popular, groundbreaking course. He has subsequently written several best-selling books and in 2011 co-founded Potentialife with Angus Ridgway, a company that provides leadership programs based on the science of behavioral change to organizations, schools and sports organizations globally.

Task 1   Summarizing

Directions: Please sum up Tal Ben-Shahar's Hamburger Model of Happiness with the guideline of the form below.

Type of Hamburger	Archetype of Person	Present Benefit	Future Benefit
Vegetarian	Rat Racer	– (less tasty)	+ (healthy)
Junk Food	Hedonist (享乐主义者)	+ (tasty)	– (unhealthy)
Worst	Nihilism (虚无主义)	– (tasteless)	– (unhealthy)
Ideal	Happiness	+ (tasty)	+ (healthy)
Outline: 1. Which type of person is compared to each kind of hamburger? 2. What are the main features of each type of person?			

Unit 3

Task 2 Synthesizing Information

Directions: The audio clip and the video clip in Part One, Text A, and Text B all express the views of the authors on happiness. Please work in groups to complete the table below, summarizing their views and noting the sources. An example is already done for you. Please report the results of your group to the class.

Authors	Main Idea	Sources / Academic Fields
AARP Research Center	The AARP carried out a research on what defines happiness for Americans between the ages of 35 and 80 through the poll conducted in 2012. The results showed that important factors affecting people's happiness, content and fulfillment were health, family, wealth, and ages. Key findings are included: Most Americans ages 35+ are happy. There is a U-shaped happiness curve; but early 50s is the lowest point of well being. Regardless of age, good relationship with friends, family and even pets are found to be universally important and the key driver of happiness. Health is a universal enabler of happiness; without health, it is difficult to achieve happiness. Income matters, but does not guarantee happiness.	audio; sociology
Graham Hill	Hill advocated his philosophy of less stuff and more happiness. _____ _____	video; environment protection, architecture and design
Aristotle	Aristotle firstly argues that _____ _____ _____	classic works; ancient Greek philosophy
Tal Ben-Shahar	Tal Ben-Shahar developed a unique model of happiness known as "The Hamburger Model." _____ _____	popular works; positive psychology

Task 3 Making Comments

Directions: Please give an oral presentation to comment on the hamburger model of happiness. You may first state your view on one of the four archetypes and then support your view with convincing examples. Try to use proper transitions for the process description.

Tips

RAT RACER: Write about a period in your life when you felt as if you were running on a treadmill, living as a rat racer, for the future. Why were you doing what you were doing? What, if any, were some of the benefits of living that way? What, if any, price did you pay?

2. HEDONIST: Describe a period in your life when you lived as a hedonist or engaged in hedonistic experiences. What, if any, were some of the benefits of living that way? What, if any, price did you pay?
3. NIHILIST: Write about a particularly difficult experience during which you felt nihilistic, or about a longer period of time during which you felt helpless. Describe your deepest feelings and your deepest thoughts, which you experienced then as well as what come up as you are writing.
4. HAPPY: Describe an extremely happy period in your life or a particularly happy experience. In your imagination, transport yourself to that time, try to re-experience the emotions, and then write about them.

Part Four Cross Cultural Communication

Passage A

获得相对幸福和绝对幸福的方法

冯友兰

《庄子》第一篇题为《逍遥游》,这篇文章纯粹是一些解人颐的故事。这些故事所含的思想是,获得幸福有不同等级。自由发展我们的自然本性,可以使我们得到一种相对幸福;绝对幸福是通过对事物的自然本性有更高一层的理解而得到的。

这些必要条件的第一条是自由发展我们的自然本性,为了实现这一条,必须充分自由发挥我们自然的能力。这种能力就是我们的"德","德"是直接从"道"来的。庄子对于道、德的看法同老子的一样。例如他说:"泰初有无。无有无名,一之所起。有一而未形。物得以生谓之德。"(《庄子·天地》)所以我们的"德",就是使我们成为我们者。我们的这个"德",即自然能力,充分而自由地发挥了,也就是我们的自然本性充分而自由地发展了,这个时候我们就是幸福的……

万物的自然本性不同,其自然能力也各不相同。可是有一点是共同的,就是在它们充分而自由地发挥其自然能力的时候,它们即是同等地幸福。《逍遥游》里讲了一个大鸟和小鸟的故事。两只鸟的能力完全不一样。大鸟能飞九万里,小鸟从这棵树飞不到那棵树。可是只要它们都做到了它们能做的,爱做的,它们都同样地幸福。所以万物的自然本性没有绝对的同,也不必有绝对的同。

获得绝对幸福的方法

可是道家思想还有另一个方向,它强调万物自然本性的相对性,以及人与宇宙的"同一"。要达到这种"同一",人需要更高层次的知识和理解。由这种同一所得到的幸福才是真正的绝对幸福,《庄子》的《逍遥游》里讲明了这种幸福。

在这一篇里,描写了大鸟、小鸟的幸福之后,庄子说有个人名叫列子,能够乘风而行。"彼于致福者,未数数然也。此虽免乎行,犹有所待者也。"他所待者就是风,由于他必须依赖风,所以他的幸福在这个范围里还是相对的。接着庄子问道:"若夫乘天地之正而御六气之辩,以游无穷者,彼且恶乎待哉?故曰;至人无己,神人无功,圣人无名。"

庄子在这里描写的就是已经得到绝对幸福的人。他是至人,神人,圣人。他绝对幸福,因为他超越了事物的普通区别。他也超越了自己与世界的区别,"我"与"非我"的区别。所以他无己。他与道合一。道无为而无不为。道无为,所以无功。圣人与道合一,所以也无功。他也许治天下,但是他的治就是只让人们听其自然,不加干涉,让每个人充分地、自由地发挥他自己的自然能力。道无名,圣人与道合一,所以也无名。

(938 字)

注解

1. 本篇节选于《中国哲学简史》(*A Short History of Chinese Philosophy*),冯友兰(Fung Yu-lan)著英文版,纽约麦克米伦公司出版,1947年;涂又光译,北京大学出版社,2013年,103—108页。冯先生于1946年受宾西法尼亚大学之邀,赴美讲学期间用英文写出了一部《中国哲学简史》。该书的思想,语言风格及文化、哲学涵蕴别具风采,深受外国读者欢迎,先后有法、意、日、韩等12种语言的译本出版,可谓中国学术史上的一大奇观。

2. 冯友兰(1895年—1990年),字芝生,河南唐河县人。中国当代著名哲学家、哲学史家、教育家。1915年自中国公学考入北京大学哲学门,学习中国哲学。1920年留学美国哥伦比亚大学研究院,师从杜威先生学习西方哲学,1923年毕业回国。1926年任燕京大学教授。1928年起,任清华大学哲学系教授兼哲学系主任、文学院院长、校秘书长、校务会议主席等职。20世纪30年代初,在燕京大学任教时完成了两卷本《中国哲学史》,成为大学的教科书。冯先生在哲学教育和创造领域辛勤耕耘了六十余年,培养了一代代的哲学家、哲学史家,为中国哲学史的学科建设做出了重大贡献。

Word Bank

获得相对幸福的方法	way of Achieving Relative Happiness
获得绝对幸福的方法	way of Achieving Absolute Happiness
《庄子》	*The Chuang-tzu*
《逍遥游》	*The Happy Excursion*
自由发展我们的自然本性	a free development of our natures
德	Te
道	Tao
与道合一	the one with the Tao
道无为而无不为。	The Tao does nothing and yet there is nothing that is not done.
道无名。	The Tao is nameless.

Directions: Please summarize the passage in English. Your summary should be about 150—200 words. The word bank above may give you some help.

_____
_____
_____
_____
_____
_____
_____
_____
_____
_____

Passage B

Platonic Harmony

Nicholas White

To many philosophers, the obvious way to react to the plurality of considerations and their potential conflicts, as so far described, is to think that happiness must be a *harmony* of aims, etc. This was certainly Plato's view. Indeed, he seems to have thought it unavoidable. In his description of "the completely good man" (*The Republic*, 427e; 柏拉图著《理想国》), he describes the harmony of such a person's soul or personality. Such a person

> *doesn't allow any part of himself to do the work of another part, or let the various elements in him interfere with each other. He organizes what's really his own well, and rules himself. He puts himself in order, is his own friend, and harmonizes the … parts of himself like … limiting notes in a musical chord. He binds those parts together, and any others in between, and from having been many he becomes entirely one, moderate and harmonious. (Rep. 443d)*

Plato's thinking is guided by two considerations, both of which turned out to be highly influential. One was the thought that a conflict among aims is bad for a person. The other was that unless happiness is some kind of harmony, no clear account of it can be articulated or understood.

On the first point, Plato's reasons were these: In the first place, he thought, a person whose aims aren't consistent is doomed to frustration. That's of course because if two aims can't be satisfied together, then one of them will be frustrated. And frustration is normally bad. Thus Plato describes the "prison house" in which the "tyrannical" personality "is pent, being... filled with multitudinous and manifold terrors and appetites … greedy and avid of spirit as he is" *(Rep. 579b)*. The tyrant's unhappiness is brought about largely by his having desires that stand in each other's way.

Second, Plato believed that conflict within a person's soul betokens a failure of some of its parts to perform their "natural function." Plato believed that each element of a human personality has a function that it naturally performs. Hunger, for instance, has the natural function of causing an intake of food that will keep the body in good condition. However, the "bodily" desires tend to encroach on each other. For example, a glutton's desire to eat might move him to forgo exercise, and so no longer be in good shape. Plato seems to hold that the performance of natural function is a good thing.

Third, Plato holds that if a person is subject to conflict, then that's generally because his reason hasn't successfully governed his personality. In particular his reason hasn't governed and organized his desires. In that case, not only is his reason not performing its natural function—which is to organize and direct the personality—but in addition, *that* means (Plato believes) that the person's reason doesn't have a clear, consistent conception of the harmony of all desires to which a person should conform. That's a failure of reason, a kind of irrationality.

This last point makes it clear why Plato thought that unless happiness is a harmony of aims, no intelligible account of it can be given—by a philosopher or anybody else.

Like many philosophers, Plato assumes that the whole point of articulating the concept of happiness is to give people guidance. I've already pointed out that we can think of the concept as arising from our efforts to deliberate about what to do. The concept of happiness is the analogue, writ large, of what we do when we plan for the short run. So, it seems to follow, an account of happiness ought to be usable as a guide. It ought, that is, to guide us through the uncertainties that we encounter when we think about our various sometimes conflicting aims and desires. It ought to tell us what to do when they give contrary instructions.

If the concept of happiness is to be such a guide, it seems also to follow that it must specify a consistent set of aims. If you're told to do A and B but they can't both be done, then you haven't been told what to do. You've got to decide on your own whether to do A or B or for that matter something else. So it appears that a conflicting specification of aims can't articulate what happiness is, if it's to do its job of guiding. That makes it useless for the philosopher or anyone else to offer it. That's how Plato reasons.

That's exactly the reason why Plato rejected Gorgias' account of happiness as "getting what(ever) you want." If that's what Gorgias tells you to do, and if your wants are inconsistent as most people's are, then Gorgias hasn't after all made a recommendation that's coherent and that you could follow. That's the position that Callicles is in. If he itches for his whole life and wants to scratch, Gorgias' view tells him to scratch, and that that's "the greatest good." But Callicles doesn't think that being in that state is a good thing.

(847 words)

Notes

1. The passage was abridged from *A Brief History of Happiness,* written by Nicholas White, first published in 2006 by Blackwell Publishing Ltd. In this brief history, philosopher Nicholas White reviews 2,500 years of philosophical thought about happiness. It addresses key questions such as: What is happiness? Should happiness play such a dominant role in our lives? How can we deal with conflicts between the various things that make us happy? It considers the ways in which major thinkers from antiquity to the modern day have treated happiness: from Plato's notion of the harmony of the soul (柏拉图的内心和谐观), through to Nietzsche's championing of conflict over harmony (尼采的内心冲突观). And it also

relates questions about happiness to ethics and to practical philosophy.
2. Nicholas P. White is Professor Emeritus of Philosophy at the University of California, Irvine, USA.
http://www.thenile.com.au/books/Nicholas-White/A-Brief-History-of-Happiness/9781405115209/
3. Gorgias was a Greek sophist, pre-Socratic philosopher and rhetorician. 高尔吉亚（前 483—前 375 年，古希腊哲学家、修辞学家）
4. Callicles（卡利克勒斯，c.484—late 5th century BCE) was an ancient Athenian political philosopher best remembered for his role in Plato's dialogue *Gorgias*, where he "presents himself as a no-holds-barred, bare-knuckled, clear-headed advocate of Realpolitik."

Directions: Please summarize the passage in Chinese. Your summary should be about 200—300 words.

Unit 4

ARCHITECTURE OF THE WORLD

Among the family of architecture of the world, Chinese architecture may be considered an independent branch by itself. Its history is as long as the history of Chinese civilization.

From every source of information—literary, graphical and exemplary—there can be gathered evidences testifying to the fact that the Chinese people have always employed an indigenous system of construction and a conception of planning which have retained their principal characteristics from the earliest times till the present day.

—From "General Characteristics", Chapter One of *Chinese Architecture: Art and Artifacts* by Liang Sicheng

Learning Objectives

Upon completion of this unit, you should be able to:

Remember & Understand	★ recognize and interpret architectural terms; ★ identify and explain in your own words the thesis and the major points of Text A and Text B;
Analyze & Apply	★ use root words to make new words; ★ make reference to the thesis and the major points of Text A and Text B in your writing; ★ learn to write sentences with attributive clause, both defining attributive clauses and non-defining attributive clauses;
Evaluate & Create	★ write with the help of sketches/illustrative pictures; ★ synthesize information concerning architecture of different styles and different times; ★ deliver a clear and coherent oral presentation of your view on how to be a great architect.

Part One Lead-in

Section 1 Listening

Task 1 Filling in the Blanks

Directions: Please fill in the blanks with one or two words on the basis of what you have heard in the listening passage.

Generally speaking, there were about seven major independent architectural systems in the ancient world. Some of them have long ceased to exist, or have not been ____1____, such as ancient Egyptian, West Asian, Indian and American structures. Only Chinese, European and Islamic structures are considered to be the world's three ____2____. The Chinese and European structures continued over the longest period of time and spread over the widest area and consequently, produced more ____3____.

During the 3,000 years of the feudalist society, Chinese ancient architecture formulated gradually its unique system, coupled with a considerable progress in urban planning, garden designing, and house ____4____. In 221 B.C., the First Emperor of the Qin Empire mobilized the resources of the country to do construction works on ____5____, including A'Fang Palace, the Great Wall and the Dujiangyan ____6____. From then on, many more massive construction works of lasting fame were carried out in the history of China.

The Forbidden City was the Chinese ____7____ from the Ming dynasty to the end of the Qing dynasty. For almost 500 years, it served as the home of emperors and their households, as well as the ____8____ of Chinese government. Built in 1406 to 1420, the complex consists of 980 buildings and covers 180 acres. The palace complex exemplifies ____9____, and has influenced cultural and architectural developments in East Asia and elsewhere. The Forbidden City was declared ____10____ in 1987, and is listed by UNESCO as the largest collection of preserved ancient wooden structures in the world.

Task 2 Group Discussion

Directions: Please discuss the following questions in pairs or groups based on what you have heard.

1. What are the seven major independent architectural systems of the ancient world? How much do you know about them?
2. Which architecture style do you like, Chinese style or western style? Why?
3. Can you describe one famous Chinese architecture or an architecture in your hometown?

Section 2 Watching

Task 1 Group Discussion

Directions: Please watch the video "The Great Pyramid of Egypt" and discuss the following questions in pairs or groups.

1. Why do people think pyramids were committed to the quest for eternity?
2. What do you know about the first true smooth sided pyramids?
3. How long did the period of amazing technological progress of building the pyramids last? What caused the loss of secrets of the pyramid's construction?

Task 2   Blank Filling

Directions: Please watch the video again, and pay attention to the last part about the research of methods of building the pyramids. Fill in the blanks.

But none of this fascinating research yielded any new information about the methods used to build the pyramids, especially not for the biggest and most complex of them all, Khufu. Towering at 146 meters, it was the tallest _____1_____ ever built until the end of the 19th century. Khufu is also the only pyramid with a _____2_____ tucked away at its heart. With beams weighing over 60 tons, a genuine challenge within the challenge.

The pyramid's _____3_____ are the two key mysteries surrounding Khufu's construction. Nobody until now has ever solved this riddle written in stone. Still, many theories have been put forward. In the 5th century BC, the Greek historian, Herodotus, suggested the use of _____4_____. Egyptologists then imagined massive ramps leading up to the summit, or else _____5_____. But in the end, these theories, which we find in every historical reference book, have never been very convincing.

Part Two   Reading and Writing

Text A

In Search of Ancient Chinese Architecture
Liang Sicheng

For the last nine years, the Institute for Research in Chinese Architecture, of which I am a member, has been *dispatching* twice every year, on trips of two or three months' duration, small teams of field-workers, headed by a research fellow, to comb the country for ancient monuments. The ultimate aim is the *compilation* of a history of Chinese architecture, a subject that has been virtually untouched by scholars in the past. We could find little or no material in books. We have had to hunt for actual *specimens*.

We have, up till today, covered more than two hundred counties in fifteen provinces and have studied more than two thousand monuments. As head of the section of technical studies, I was able to visit most of these places personally. We are very far from our goal yet, but we have found materials of great significance which may be of interest to the general reader.

Unlike European architecture, which uses stone as its principal material, Chinese architecture is essentially of wood, a much more easily *perishable* material. Even structures in masonry（砖石建筑）are mere imitations of wooden forms in brick or stone. A student must therefore, first of all, familiarize himself with the wooden structural system. It is like learning the *Vignola*, a necessary step before one can proceed with the study of European architecture. In field work, too, the student must pay the greatest attention to wooden structures. He is actually racing with time, for these structures are all the while undergoing a steady and uncompromising process of *disintegration*. Waves of new influences, *stirring up* the strange ideas of a few men in a conservative town, can innocently *deface* a masterpiece by their efforts at so-called "modernization" of an "old-fashioned" structure. Delicate window traceries（窗饰）, finely carved door-panels, are always among the first to suffer such heartless *outrages*. Seldom does one find *to one's satisfaction* a real gem left in peace and beauty by nature and man alike. A *stray* spark from an *incense* stick may also *reduce* a whole temple *to* ashes.

4   Besides, there was the threat of a Japanese war, such an *uncalled-for* instance of human cruelty and destructive ability. The love and preservation of *antiquity* were no business of the Japanese warlords, though their nationals normally should share with us the special love and respect for our old culture from which they derived their own. Even as early as 1931 and 1932, most of my trips were abruptly *disrupted* by the renewed booms of Japanese guns, each time drawing nearer than the last, *meaning business*. It was quite evident that the days we could work in North China were limited. Before we were prevented from doing so, we decided to put our entire effort in that part of the country. The once cheerless prescience（预感）has been now, for almost three-and-half years, a painful fact. With the Institute physically removed to the far corner of China's southwest, recollections of field work over now enemy-*trodden* northern lands are the more vivid and dear with our ever increasing *nostalgia* and concern.

5   Every season's trip was *preceded* by careful preparations in library research. Books on history, geography, and *Buddhism* yielded a list of places where we hoped to find something. An *itinerary* was made up from the list for the team to follow on its field trips. Every item on the list had to be located, identified, and, if still existing, measured and photographed.

6   The finds of our trips were numerous and of varied degrees of interest and significance. Often we got from literary sources wonderful visions of certain old monuments, *only to* find, after hundreds of miles of anticipatory *pilgrimage*, a heap of ruins, with perhaps a few roof-*tiles* and stone column-bases for reward.

7   Our trips themselves were also adventures full of unexpected *ups and downs*. With physical discomfort taken for granted, we enjoyed frequently unforgettable experiences of rare charm and delight. Generally, the journeys, like odd kinds of picnics *prolonged*, were either extremely disconcerting（窘迫的）or highly entertaining when we encountered comical but disastrous misfortunes.

8   Unlike the highly expensive *expeditions* of *archaeologists*, big game hunters, or any tropical or arctic scientific explorers, the equipment for our trips was *scanty*. Besides instruments for surveying and photographing, our luggage consisted mostly of *gadgets*

of the home-made order, designed and modified by our members as they accumulated experience. Knapsacks like an electrician's, to be carried while working *perched precariously* on top of any part of a building, were among our favorite treasures, which included anything from a spool(线轴)of string to a telescopic pole that could be extended like a long, rigid fishing-rod. We, following the philosophy of the famous white knight in *Alice's Wonderland*, believed that one never knows what will prove to be useful in case of emergency, so were willing to fall off horses' backs for our burdens.

Often we had to make camp, cook, eat, and sleep under such very different circumstances each day and night and our means of transportation were so uncertain, ranging from the most ancient and *quaint* to the more usual and up-to-date, that what we considered essentials could not help being peculiar, resilient(有弹力的)tin-cans of one sort or another.

Aside from architecture, we often *came across* subjects of artistic and ethnological (民族学的)interest—handicrafts of different localities, archaic(古老的)*dramatics* of out-of-the-way towns, *queer* customs, picturesque fairs, etc, but economy of film often prevented me from photographing liberally pictures of them. On most of my trips, I was accompanied by my wife, herself an architect. But being also a writer and lover of dramatic art, she, more often than I, let her attention stray and enthusiastically insisted on some subjects for the camera at any cost. I was always glad after we returned from a trip to have the valuable pictures of scenes and buildings which would otherwise have been neglected.

(980 words)

New Words

dispatch	[dɪˈspætʃ]	v.	to send sth., esp. goods or a message, somewhere for a particular purpose 派遣,派送
compilation	[ˌkɒmpɪˈleɪʃən]	n.	the act of compiling sth. 编纂,编辑
specimen	[ˈspesəmɪn]	n.	sth. shown or examined as an example; a typical example 样本,标本
perishable	[ˈperɪʃəbl]	a.	(of sth. abstract) having a brief life or significance; transitory 易消亡的,不经久的
disintegration	[dɪˌsɪntɪˈgreɪʃən]	n.	(the act of) becoming weaker or being destroyed by breaking into small pieces 分解,分化,分裂
deface	[dɪˈfeɪs]	v.	to damage and spoil the appearance of sth. by writing or drawing on it; to damage 损坏……的外观;损坏
outrage	[ˈaʊtreɪdʒ]	n.	a shocking, morally unacceptable and usually violent action 暴行;(道义上)难以接受的事情
stray	[streɪ]	a.	having moved apart from similar things and are not in

			their expected or intended place 零星的，零落的
incense	['ɪnsens]	n.	a substance that is burnt to produce a sweet smell, esp. as part of a religious ceremony（尤指在宗教仪式上焚烧的）香
uncalled-for	[ʌn'kɔ:ldfɔ]	a.	describes a criticism, insult, remark or action that is unfair, rude or hurtful（批评、侮辱、言论或行动）不公允的；不恰当的
antiquity	[æn'tɪkwɪti]	n.	sth. of great age 古物，古董，古迹
disrupt	[dɪs'rʌpt]	v.	to prevent sth., esp. a system, process or event, from continuing as usual or as expected 打断，中断
tread	[tred]	v.	(trod, trodden/ trod) to put your foot on sth. or to press sth. down with your foot 踩，踏
nostalgia	[nɒs'tældʒə]	n.	a feeling of pleasure and sometimes slight sadness at the same time as you think about things that happened in the past 对往事的怀念，怀旧
precede	[prɪ'si:d]	v.	to be or go before sth. or sb. in time or space（指时间或空间上）处在……之前，先于
Buddhism	['bʊdɪzəm]	n.	a religion that originally comes from India, and teaches that personal spiritual improvement will lead to escape from human suffering 佛教
itinerary	[aɪ'tɪnərəri]	n.	a detailed plan or route of a journey 旅行计划，预订行程
pilgrimage	['pɪlgrɪmɪdʒ]	n.	a special journey made by a pilgrim 朝圣
tile	[taɪl]	n.	a thin, usually square or rectangular, piece of baked clay, plastic, etc. used for covering roofs, floors, walls etc. 瓦片，瓷砖
prolong	[prə'lɒŋ]	v.	to make sth. last a longer time 延长，拖延
expedition	[ˌekspə'dɪʃən]	n.	an organized journey for a particular purpose 远征；探险；考查
archaeologist	[ˌɑ:ki'ɒlədʒɪst]	n.	sb. who studies the buildings, graves, tools and other objects of people who lived in the past 考古学家
scanty	['skænti]	a.	smaller in size or amount than is considered necessary or is hoped for 不足的，缺乏的
gadget	['gædʒɪt]	n.	a small device or machine with a particular purpose 小器具，小装置，小玩意儿
perch	[pɜ:tʃ]	v.	to sit on or near the edge of sth. 坐在……（的边缘）上，栖息于
precariously	[prɪ'keərɪəsli]	ad.	in a way that is likely to fall, be damaged 不牢靠地，不稳地
quaint	[kweɪnt]	a.	old-fashioned and strange 古雅的；奇怪的
dramatics	[drə'mætɪks]	n.	theatrical performances 戏剧表演

queer	[kwɪər]	a.	strange, unusual, or not expected 怪异的，古怪的

Phrases & Expressions

stir up	to cause an unpleasant emotion or problem to begin or grow 激起（不快的情感）；挑起，煽动（事端）
to sb.'s satisfaction	in a way that a particular person feels pleased or satisfied with 使满意地
reduce sth. to sth.	to cause sth., esp. a large structure, to be destroyed and broken into pieces 将（尤指大型建筑物）彻底摧毁，将……夷为平地
mean business	to want very much to achieve sth., even if other people disagree with you 决心要做成（某事）
only to do sth.	used to show that sth. is surprising or unexpected 不料却，没想到却
ups and downs	a mixture of good and bad things 盛衰，沉浮
come across	to find sth. by chance 偶然发现，碰见

Proper Noun

Vignola	维诺拉（意大利建筑师，五柱式建筑的创造者）

1. The text is an excerpt from "In Search of Ancient Architecture in North China," Chapter Four of the book *Chinese Architecture: Art and Artifacts*. The book is a compilation of essays by Liang Sicheng in 1930's and 1940's. All the essays are about his research in Chinese ancient architecture: Chinese Architecture; A Han Terra-cotta Model of a Three-storey House; Two Liao Structure of Tu-lo Ssu, Chi Hsien; In Search of Ancient Architecture in North China; Buddhist Cave Sculpture; Five Early Chinese Pagodas; Chinese Oldest Wooden Structure; Art and Architecture—China: Arts, Language, and Mass Media.

2. The author of the book, Liang Sicheng (20 April 1901—9 January 1972), was a Chinese architect and the author of China's first modern history on Chinese architecture and founder of the Architecture Department of Northeastern University in 1928 and Tsinghua University in 1946. In early years, he studied at the University of Pennsylvania in the United States and returned to China in 1928. He was the Chinese representative in the Design Board which designed the United Nations headquarters in New York. He, along with his wife Lin Huiyin (a Chinese architect and poet), Mo Zongjiang, and Ji Yutang, discovered and analyzed the

first and second oldest timber structures still standing in China. He is recognized as the "Father of Modern Chinese Architecture."

Task 1   Generating the Outline

Directions: Please identify the thesis of the passage and the main point of each part and find out how these points develop the thesis. You may use the table below to help you.

The thesis:	The history of Chinese architecture was a subject that had never been touched by scholars in the past. The author, together with his colleagues in _____,_____ decided to go on field trips every year to hunt for _____ by themselves. Their trips were always hard ones.
Paras. 1—2: **The introduction:**	An introduction to their field work and its final aim: the compilation of _____.
Para. 3: **The urgency for their work:**	There was an urgency in searching for ancient Chinese architecture because it was a race with _____. Chinese architecture is essentially of wood, an easily _____.
Para. 4: **The Japanese war's influence:**	The Japanese war added more difficulties in their field work in North China and they had to remove to _____.
Paras. 5—10: **A description of their field trips:**	***Before the trips:*** Careful preparations in library research to make up itineraries for the team to _____. ***During the trips:*** 1) The finds of their trips: _____. 2) The trips: adventures full of _____. 3) The equipment for their trips: scanty—consisted mostly of _____ _____. 4) Their means of transportation: uncertain, ranging from _____ _____. ***After the trips:*** The author always felt glad that his wife had taken valuable pictures of _____ _____.

Task 2   Understanding the Text

Directions: Please answer the following questions based on Text A.

1. Why does the author say they have had to hunt for actual specimens of ancient Chinese monuments (Para. 1)

2. According to the author, what's the difference between European architecture and Chinese architecture (Para. 3)

3. Why does the author say they are racing with time in hunting for ancient Chinese architecture? (Para. 3)
4. Why couldn't the author and his colleagues do their field work in North China any longer? (Para. 4)
5. What did they have to do before their trip? (Para. 5)
6. Why did they often feel disappointed after they got to their destinations in searching for old monuments? (Para. 6)
7. What do we know about their trips? Please exemplify them in a logical order. (Paras. 7&9)
8. Why did they always bring with them so many different kinds of things in their knapsacks during the trips? (Para. 8)
9. Why did the author and his wife act differently in terms of photographing during their trips? What do you learn from the couple's anecdote? (Para. 10)
10. Could you use your own words to describe the work and the contribution of the author and his colleagues in searching for ancient Chinese architecture?

Task 3 Vocabulary Building

Directions: Study the following five frequently used word roots and review the words you've learnt by adding prefixes or suffixes to the roots. Examples are provided.

> -ject- = throw, cast;   -miss-, -mit = send, cast;   -solv-, -solu-, -solut = loosen
> trans-①表示"横过,越过"②表示"变换,改变,转移";   dur=last, hard

1. -ject- = throw, cast, 表示"投掷,扔"

adjective	a.	附加的(ad增加+ject+ive→扔上去的→附加的)
abject	a.	可怜的;颓丧的(ab向下+ject→向下扔→情绪颓丧的)
conjecture	n.	推测,猜想(con共同+ject+ure→大家一起扔[思想]→推测)
deject	v.	使沮丧(de向下+ject→情绪向下扔→沮丧)
dejected	a.	情绪低落的(deject+ed)
eject	v.	喷出;驱逐(e出+ject→扔出→喷出)
ejection	n.	喷出;排出物(eject+ion)
interjection	n.	感叹词(inter在中间+ject+ion→在句子中扔出的字→感叹词)
inject	v.	注射(in进+ject→扔进去→注射)
object	n./v.	物体;目标;反对(ob反+ject→反着扔→反对,引申为扔向目标)
objection	n.	反对(object反对+ion)
objective	a./n.	客观的;目标(object+ive)
project	v./n.	投射;设计;目标(pro向前+ject→向前扔→目标;项目)
projection	n.	投射;放映(project+ion)
projectile	n.	抛射物;导弹(project+ile 物体→向前扔的物体)
reject	v.	拒绝,驳回(re回+ject→扔回来→拒绝)
rejection	n.	拒绝(reject+ion)
subject	a./n.	服从的;主题(sub在……下面+ject→扔下去→服从的;扔下去让大家讨论的主题)

subjection	n.	服从,臣服(subject+ion)
subjectivity	n.	主观性(subject 主观+ivity)
trajectory	n.	弹道,轨道(tra 穿过+ject+ory→扔进去→弹道)

2. -miss-, -mit = send, cast, 表示"送,放出"

| admit | v. | 许可入学等;承认(ad+mit→送来→许可进入) |
| commission | n. | 委员会;委任(com 共同＋miss+ion→共同送出[选出]的人→委员会) |

3. -solv-, -solu-, -solut = loosen, 表示"松开"

| absolute | a. | 绝对的;无限制的(ab 不+solute→决不松开→绝对的) |
| resolve | v. | 解决(困难)(re 再+solve→再松开→解决) |

4. trans-

① 表示"横过,越过"

| transect | v. | 横切,横断(trans+sect 切→横切) |

② 表示"变换,改变,转移"

| transaction | n. | 交易;办理(trans+action 行动→交换行动→交易) |

5. dur = last, hard, 表示"持久,坚硬"

| duration | n. | 持续时间(dur+ation) |
| endure | v. | 持久,耐久(en 进入+dure 进入持久→耐久) |

Task 4　Learning the Phrases

Directions: Please fill in the blanks in the sentences below with the phrases listed in the box. Change the forms necessary. Notice that some phrases need to be used more than once.

| stir up | mean business | ups and downs | only to find |
| come across | reduce sth. to | to sb.'s satisfaction | take for granted |

1. During the bid submission stage, the bid inviting party asked the structure designer several technica questions, which he answered _____.

2. When I read a book about Ieoh Ming Pei, the great Chinese-born American architect, I _____ a sentence from him, "Strong confidence is very important in doing anything well. You mu trust yourself." His words have encouraged me a lot and will motivate me to go farther in my li journey.

3. What the senior government official said last week has _____ ethnic tension in th region. We'll see more conflicts there.

4. We ride them every day but do we ever take much notice? Well, Miha Tamura is one person wh is paying attention to escalators and that's why she started Tokyo Escalator, an online collectio of images of the moving staircases that we _____ in our daily lives.

5. Obviously I wanted to finish the book _____ and I also didn't want to disappoi people by missing the deadline.

6. There is nothing worse than trying to relax and eat a special meal _____ clouds of cigarette smoke drifting over you.
7. The _____ of life may seem unpredictable. But there are clear patterns that almost all people share. Even if you've passed your "best," you still have other good years to come. Certain important highpoints come later in life.
8. Mr. Lee said he would major in architecture and no one believed him because he was not good at painting at all. But he was determined and he _____ this time.
9. In fact, holding positive thoughts in the mind to try to counter negative feeling energies in the subconscious will only _____ those negative feelings and attract more negativity! Negative feelings must be released directly by some kind of process based on a sophisticated understanding of how the subconscious works.
10. Having suffered from a massive earthquake and been _____ ruins, the city now is taking on a new look after magnificent reconstruction.

Task 5 Studying the Sentence Structure
Attributive Clause
Sentences from the text
1. For the last nine years, the Institute for Research in Chinese Architecture, <u>of which I am a member</u>, has been dispatching twice every year, on trips of two or three months' duration, small teams of field-workers, headed by a research fellow, to comb the country for ancient monuments. (Para. 1)
2. The love and preservation of antiquity were no business of the Japanese warlords, though their nationals normally should share with us the special love and respect for our old culture <u>from which they derived their own</u>. (Para. 4)

Directions: Please follow the examples in the text and create two sentences with attributive clause on your own.
Tips

> 1. Attributive clause is a sentence that is used to modify a noun or a pronoun, called antecedents in attributive clause, and this noun or pronoun will take up a certain place in the attributive clause, such as a subject, an object, etc.
> 2. According to the function of the attributive clauses, the sentences can be divided into two types: sentences with defining attributive clauses and sentences with non-defining attributive clauses.
> 3. Place commas in the non-defining attributive clauses, but do not place commas in defining attributive clauses.

Task 6 Paraphrasing Difficult Sentences

1. Waves of new influences, stirring up the strange ideas of a few men in a conservative town, can innocently deface a masterpiece by their efforts at so-called "modernization" of an "old-fashioned" structure.

2. Even as early as 1931 and 1932, most of my trips were abruptly disrupted by the renewed booms of Japanese guns, each time drawing nearer than the last, meaning business.

3. Often we got from literary sources wonderful visions of certain old monuments, only to find, after hundreds of miles of anticipatory pilgrimage, a heap of ruins, with perhaps a few roof-tiles and stone column-bases for reward.

4. We, following the philosophy of the famous white knight in *Alice's Wonderland*, believed that one never knows what will prove to be useful in case of emergency, so were willing to fall off horses' backs for our burdens.

5. Our means of transportation were so uncertain, ranging from the most ancient and quaint to the more usual and up-to-date, that what we considered essentials could not help being peculiar, resilient tin-cans of one sort or another.

Task 7 Summarizing the Text

Directions: Please summarize Text A in about 100 words. You may use the table in Task 1 to help you.

Task 8 Writing with the Help of Sketches/Illustrative Pictures

Directions: A sketch/illustrative picture is a drawing that is done quickly without a lot of details. It can provide a visual aid to your description and make it more comprehensible. Now, write a passage about a well-known architecture in the world according to your knowledge of it (its history, design, development, story, etc). You can use the sketch/illustrative picture provided to help you when you come to the part of describing it. Your writing should be about 200 words. You may use what is provided in the box below to help you.

Example:

Big Ben is the nickname for...
The tower was completed in 1858 and...
The tower has become one of the most...
The bottom 200 feet of the tower's structure consists of...
The remainder of the tower's height is...
The interior volume of the tower is...
Due to changes in ground conditions since construction...

Sample Writing:

Big Ben is the nickname for the Great Bell of the clock at the north end of the Palace of Westminster in London, and is often extended to refer to the clock and the clock tower. The tower is officially known as the Elizabeth Tower, renamed as such to celebrate the Diamond Jubilee of Elizabeth II in 2012 (prior to 2012 it was known as simply "Clock Tower"). The tower was completed in 1858 and it holds the second largest four-faced chiming clock in the world. The tower has become one of the most prominent symbols of the United Kingdom and is often in the establishing shot of films set in London.

The bottom 200 feet of the tower's structure consists of brickwork with sand colored Anston limestone cladding. The remainder of the tower's height is a framed spire of cast iron. The tower is founded on a 50 feet square raft, made of 10 feet thick concrete, at a depth of 13 feet below ground level. The four clock dials are 180 feet above ground. The interior volume of the tower is 164,200 cubic feet. Due to changes in ground conditions since construction, the tower leans slightly to the north-west, by roughly 230 millimeters over 55 meters height, giving an inclination of approximately 1/240. The tower has no lift, so people have to climb the 334 limestone stairs to the top.

(231 words)

Your Task:

> The Temple of Heaven (天坛) is a complex of religious buildings...
> The complex was visited by the Emperors of...
> The Hall of Prayer for Good Harvests (祈年殿) is a magnificent...
> The building is completely wooden...

Your Writing:

_____
_____
_____
_____
_____
_____
_____
_____

Part Three Reading and Speaking

Text B

The Sydney Opera House

1   The Sydney Opera House has become the international symbol of not only Sydney Harbor, but all of Australia, *outranking* such natural features as *the Great Barrier Reef, the Outback*, and *Ayres Rock* (Uluru). Even in the cultural society of opera houses, the Sydney Opera House is a star, hosting more events than any other performing arts center in the world. At the time of the Australian *Bicentennial* celebrations in 1988, Sydney Opera House was voted one of "the wonders of the 20th century".

2   However, during the building's problematic construction period, from 1959 to 1973, it was nothing of the sort. Despite the many vicissitudes (变化无常) that the structure and the plan underwent, the Opera House remains a powerful and comprehensive complex, *indelibly* tied to its dramatic site, a voluptuous (感官享受的) exciting, unique cultural flume (渠道) sitting *astride* a bedrock of *granite* on *Bennelong Point*.

In 1957, Utzon, its Danish architect, unexpectedly won the competition to design the Sydney Opera House. His *submission* was one of 233 designs from 32 countries, many of them from the most famous architects of the day. Although he had won six other architectural competitions previously, the Opera House was his first non-domestic project.

The original concept drawings *submitted* for the competition were simple and *diagrammatic*, yet profound—a portent(奇观)of a new kind of modernist architecture. The American Eero Saarinen and Britain's Leslie Martin were the two foreign architect assessors, and they saw something special in Utzon's design. All the assessors admired the "Classical" treatment of the Bennelong Point site which was to *accommodate* the massive base and to be *resurfaced* by what the judges saw as a "magnificent ceremonial approach to buildings that provided a unity for structural expression." Saarinen described it as "genius" and declared he could not *endorse* any other choice. Later he *referred to* it *as* a scheme that showed a "beautiful movement of people within that architecture."

The construction work began on 2nd March 1959. The extraordinary structure of the shells themselves represented a puzzle for the engineers. This was not resolved until 1961, when Utzon himself finally *came up with* the solution. He replaced the original elliptical(椭圆形的)shells with a design based on complex sections of a sphere. Utzon says his design was inspired by the simple act of peeling an orange: the 14 shells of the building, if combined, would form a perfect sphere.

Although Utzon had spectacular, innovative plans for the *interior* of these halls, he was unable to realize this part of his design. In mid-1965, the New South Wales Liberal government of Robert Askin was elected. Askin had been a vocal critic of the project *prior to* gaining office. His new Minister for Public Works, Davis Hughes, was even less *sympathetic*. Utzon soon found himself in conflict with the new Minister. Attempting to *rein* in the *escalating* cost of the project, Hughes began questioning Utzon's capability, his designs, schedules, and cost estimates, refusing to pay running costs. In 1966, after a final request that plywood(胶合板)manufacturer Ralph Symonds should be one of the suppliers for the roof structure was refused, Utzon resigned from the job, closed his Sydney office and *vowed* never to return to Australia. When Utzon left, the shells were almost complete, and costs *amounted to* only $22.9 million. Following major changes to the original plans for the interiors, costs finally rose to $103 million.

The Opera House was finally completed, and opened in 1973 by Elizabeth II, Queen of Australia. The architect was not invited to the ceremony, nor was his name even mentioned during any of the speeches.

Although he never went back to Australia to see his masterpiece, in 1999 Utzon was invited to work again on the Sydney Opera House. *In collaboration with* his son Jan and the Sydney architect Richard Johnson, he developed a set of design principles for future changes to the building and worked on the interior, *refurbishing* the Reception Hall and designing a wall-length tapestry(挂毯)to hang in the *foyer*. The Utzon Room, overlooking Sydney Harbor, was officially dedicated in October 2004. It is the only authentic Utzon interior in the building and was named after Utzon *in honour of* the great architect. In a statement at the time Utzon wrote: "The fact that I'm mentioned in such a marvellous way, it gives me the greatest pleasure and satisfaction. I don't think you can give me more joy as the architect. It *supersedes* any medal of any kind that I could get and have got."

Utzon's architecture was about light, sunlight and its *penetrating*, reflective qualities, as well as massive ground bases and dominating roofs that derived from his interest in the Mayan idea (*Monte Albán*, Mexico) of the earth as a ground platform and the openness above dominated by sky and clouds. Utzon himself later explained his ideas: "I had to *visualise* five to six thousand people going out to that *peninsula*, which is perhaps 600 by 300 feet, so automatically I made this peninsula into a 'rock' and put everything to do with preparation (*rehearsal* rooms, workshops, etc.) underneath the big 45ft high platform ... finished plays were presented to the audience on top of this 'rock' covered by the big sails... "

Frank Gehry, a world-famous architect, commented: "Utzon made a building well *ahead of* its *time*, far ahead of available technology, and he persevered through extraordinarily *malicious* publicity and negative criticism to build a building that changed the image of an entire country."

Utzon received many honours, including the Gold Medal Awards from the Royal Australian Institute of Architects. In 2003, the same year that Sydney Opera House celebrated its 30th birthday, Jorn Utzon was awarded the Pritzker Prize for Architecture, the highest award in its field, which is often referred to as the Nobel Prize of architecture.

In 2007 Sydney Opera House was *designated* a *UNESCO* World Heritage Site.

On 29th November 2008, Jorn Utzon died peacefully in his sleep in Copenhagen, aged 90.

(990 words)

(from http://www.csus.edu/indiv/s/shawg/idee/images/2.html, http://en.wikipedia.org/wiki/J%C3%B8rn_Utzon)

New Words

outrank	[ˌaʊtˈræŋk]	v.	to have a higher rank than...(级别、地位)比……高,在……之上

bicentennial	[ˌbaɪsenˈtenɪəl]	n.	the day or year that is 200 years after a particular (UK: bicentenary) event, especially an important one 200周年, 200周年纪念日
indelibly	[ɪnˈdelɪbli]	ad.	describes a mark or substance that is impossible to remove by washing or in any other way 洗不掉；无法去除；持久地
astride	[əˈstraɪd]	prep.	with a leg on each side of sth.; extending across 跨（或骑）在……上；跨越在……上
granite	[ˈɡrænɪt]	n.	a very hard, grey, pink and black rock, which is used for building 花岗岩，花岗石
submission	[səbˈmɪʃən]	n.	the act of giving sth. for a decision to be made by others or a document formally given in this way 提交，呈递
submit	[səbˈmɪt]	v.	to give or offer sth. for a decision to be made by others 提交，呈递
diagrammatic	[ˌdaɪəɡrəˈmætɪk]	a.	of a simple plan which represents a machine, system or idea, etc., often drawn to explain how it works; be brief 图的，图解的；概略的，梗概的
accommodate	[əˈkɒmədeɪt]	v.	to provide with a place to live or to be stored in 为……提供住宿；容纳；为……提供空间
resurface	[ˌriːˈsɜːfɪs]	v.	to put a new surface on a road 重新铺（路），给……重铺路面
endorse	[ɪnˈdɔːs]	v.	to make a public statement of your approval or support for sth. or sb. (公开) 赞同，认可，支持
interior	[ɪnˈtɪəriər]	n.	the inside part of sth. 内部
sympathetic	[ˌsɪmpəˈθetɪk]	a.	showing, esp. by what you say, that you understand; showing your support and agreement 同情的，理解的；支持的
rein	[reɪn]	v.	to keep under control 控制，约束
escalating	[ˈeskəˌleɪtɪŋ]	a.	become greater; increasing 逐步增强的；逐步上升的
vow	[vaʊ]	v.	to make a firm promise or decision to do sth. 发誓，立誓
collaboration	[kəˌlæbəˈreɪʃən]	n.	the situation of two or more people working together to create or achieve the same thing 合作，协作
refurbish	[ˌriːˈfɜːbɪʃ]	v.	to make a room or building look fresh and new again 再装修，整修，把……翻新
foyer	[ˈfɔɪər]	n.	a large, open area just inside the entrance of a public building such as a theater or hotel; lobby （剧院、宾馆等公共建筑物入口处内的）门厅

supersede	[ˌsupərˈsid]	v.	to replace sth. older, less effective, or less important 替代, 取代
penetrate	[ˈpeniˌtreit]	v.	to move into or through sth. 进入, 穿透, 渗入
visualise	[ˈvɪʒʊəlaɪz]	v.	to form a picture of sb. or sth. in your mind, in order to imagine or remember 使形象化, 使能被看见
peninsula	[pəˈnɪnsələ]	n.	an area of land mostly surrounded by water but connected to a larger piece of land 半岛
rehearsal	[rɪˈhɜːsəl]	n.	a time when all the people involved in a play, dance, etc. practise in order to prepare for a performance 排练, 排演
malicious	[məˈlɪʃəs]	a.	intended to harm or upset other people 恶意的, 恶毒的
designate	[ˈdezɪgneɪt]	v.	to say officially that a place or thing has a particular character or purpose 指定, 认定

Phrases & Expressions

refer to sth. as	call sth. as 将……称为
come up with	to suggest or think of an idea or plan 想出, 提出（主意或计划）
prior to	before a particular time or event 在……之前
rein in	to put under control 控制
amount to	to become a particular amount 合计达, 达到, 总计
in collaboration with	in cooperation with 与……合作
in honour of	in order to celebrate or show great respect for sb. or sth. 尊敬
ahead of time	earlier than a particular moment 提前

Proper Nouns

The Great Barrier Reef	（澳大利亚）大堡礁
the Outback	（尤指澳大利亚）内地
Ayres Rock (Uluru)	（位于澳大利亚中部的）艾尔斯岩, 是最著名的土著人文化遗址之一
Bennelong Point	（悉尼港）便利朗角
Monte Albán	（墨西哥）阿尔班山
UNESCO	（United Nations Educational, Scientific and Cultural Organization）联合国教科文组织

Notes

1. Jorn Utzon, (9th April 1918—29th November 2008) was a Danish architect, most notable for designing the Sydney Opera House in Australia. When it was declared a World Heritage Site on 28th June 2007, Utzon became only the second person to have received such recognition for one of his works during his lifetime. Other noteworthy works of him include Bagsværd Church near Copenhagen and the National Assembly Building in Kuwait. He also made important contributions to housing design, especially with his Kingo Houses near Helsingør.
2. The Sydney Opera House is a multi-venue performing arts centre in Sydney, New South Wales, Australia. Situated on Bennelong Point in Sydney Harbour, close to the Sydney Harbour Bridge, the facility is adjacent to the Sydney central business district and the Royal Botanic Gardens, between Sydney and Farm Coves.

Task 1　Summarizing

Directions: Please fill in the following Chronicle of Sydney Opera House. Then tell a story about this world-famous architecture in your own words.

Chronicle of Sydney Opera House

Year	Event
1957	
1959	
1961	
1965	
1966	
1973	
1988	
1999	
2003	
2004	
2007	
2008	

Task 2 Synthesizing Information

Directions: The audio clip and the video clip in Part One, Text A, and Text B all have something concerning architecture of different styles and different ages. As examples of ancient architecture, Chinese Forbidden City and Egyptian pyramids are introduced. One major difference between traditional Chinese and European architectures is explained. As one example of modern western architecture, Sydney Opera House is studied along with the story of building it. Please work in groups to complete the table below with what you've learned from this unit. Some of the information has already been given to you. Add more information after surfing the Internet. Please report the results of your group to the class.

Chinese Forbidden City	1. Built in 1406 to 1420, the Forbidden City consists of 980 buildings and covers 180 acres. 2. The Forbidden City is located in the center of Beijing, China, and now houses the Palace Museum. 3. The Forbidden City was the Chinese imperial palace from… 4. For almost 500 years, the Forbidden City served as the home of… … …
Egyptian Pyramids	1. Pyramids were the sacred gateways that let Egyptian pharaohs pass through to the land of immortal life after death. 2. The Egyptians built the finest and most impressive pyramids in a single century at the close of the prehistoric era. 3. Most were built as tombs for the country's pharaohs… 4. The first pyramids were step pyramids. The first true smooth sided pyramids were … … …
Features of Traditional Chinese and European Architectures	1. Traditionally, European architecture uses stone as its principal material while Chinese architecture is essentially of wood. 2. In historic China, architectural emphasis was laid upon the horizontal axis, in particular the construction of a heavy platform and a large roof that floats over this base, with the vertical walls not as well emphasized. This contrasts Western architecture, which tends to grow in height and depth. 3. Chinese architecture stresses… 4. Medieval architecture in Europe: … 5. Gothic architecture in Europe: … 6. Renaissance architecture in Europe: … … …

Sydney Opera House	1. The Sydney Opera House has become the international symbol of not only Sydney Harbor, but all of Australia. 2. The Sydney Opera House hosts more events than any other performing arts center in the world. 3. In 1973… 4. In 1988… 5. In 2007… … …

Task 3 Making Comments

Directions: Please study the following information about Jorn Utzon, the architect for the Sydney Opera House and then make your comment on how to be a great architect. For example, what quality and what experience should a good architect possess?

Information Pool

1. Utzon was born in Copenhagen, the son of a naval architect.
2. As a result of his family's interest in art, from 1937 he attended the Royal Danish Academy of Fine Arts.
3. Following his graduation in 1942, he joined Gunnar Asplund（20世纪上半叶极具影响力的北欧建筑师之一）in Stockholm.
4. He took a particular interest in the works of American architect Frank Lloyd Wright（20世纪美国最重要的建筑师之一）.
5. In 1946 he visited Alvar Aalto（芬兰现代建筑大师、艺术家）in Helsinki.
6. In 1947—1948 he travelled in Europe (in 1948 he went to Morocco where he was taken by the tall clay buildings).
7. In 1949, he travelled to the United States and Mexico. Fascinated by the way the Mayans built towards the sky to get closer to God, he commented that his time in Mexico was "one of the greatest architectural experiences in my life." In America, he visited Lloyd Wright's home, Taliesin West, in the Arizona desert and met Charles and Ray Eames（20世纪最有影响力的美国夫妻档设计师，是建筑、家具和工业设计等现代设计领域的先锋设计师）.
8. In 1950 he established his own studio in Copenhagen.
9. In 1957, he travelled first to China (where he was particularly interested in the Chinese desire for harmony), Japan (where he learnt much about the interaction between interiors and exteriors) and India (where the pyramids provided further inspiration), before arriving in Australia in 1957 where he stayed until 1966.
0. All above contributed to Utzon's understanding of factors which contribute to successful architectural design.

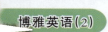

Part Four　Cross Cultural Communication

Passage A

中国建筑本土化

崔　恺

　　过往几十年,中国建筑走过了一条漫长的现代化之路,前辈们为了将传统民族风格与现代功能空间巧妙地结合起来付出了巨大的努力。有的谓之"形似",比较"显",有的谓之"神似",比较"隐"。这类优秀建筑遍布全国各地,成为那个时代的建筑艺术特征,令人尊敬。今天,我们进入了信息化时代,所有的事物似乎都可以当作信息的载体,所有的联系都可视为信息的交流。信息量之大,无所不在,信息交流之广,无所不至。就建筑而言,文化信息的表达不再是说教式的,建筑与文化的关系呈现出一种多元化景象。

　　比如说相对民族风格大而说之的概念,是不是更应强调每一个地区、每一处环境更具体的特色?比如说文化不应只是一种装饰符号,一种标签,更应强调内涵,强调深层次的文化积淀?比如说历史的本质的发展,传统的原型是创新,对历史文化的传承是不是更应强调创新和发展?比如说文化不是牵强附会的,更应强调研究它所生发的环境,而那环境也绝非静态。于是今天大家在一起,谈得更多的不再是民族风格,而是本土文化。

　　我理解本土的概念可以有几层涵义。其一是环境的概念,就是脚下的这片土地。气候的变化、河流的干枯、环境的污染、资源的消耗都和建筑密切有关,本土设计就是要担负起这样一份不可推卸的责任。其二是文化的概念,就是生长于这片沃土之上生生不息的文化,它既代表着五千年的古老文明,又呈现于今日的现代生活。本土设计,就是要扎根在这片文化的沃土中,继续创造和延续新的文化。三是空间的概念,就是建筑的地域性和场所感,建筑脱离了这种地域性,就成了流行的时装,城市中充斥着这类时装建筑,就显得浮躁而苍白。本土设计就是要创作这种地域性的建筑,让城市重新找回自身的特色,让人们重新找到自己的认同感。如今,在全球化浪潮的冲击下,在中国建筑市场日益成为国际建筑界的大舞台的今天,我以为中国建筑本土化既是保护和弘扬我们自身文化的需要,也是我们中国建筑师的立足之本。

(784 字)

 注解

1. 本篇选自崔恺的《本土设计》(Native Design),清华大学出版社 2008 年出版。
2. 作者崔恺 1957 年 8 月出生,毕业于天津大学。中国工程院土木、水利与建筑工程学部院士。现任中国建筑设计研究院副院长、院总建筑师、国家工程设计大师、中国建筑学会副理事长。

Word Bank

中国建筑	Chinese architecture	多元化景象	plural form
本土化	local concept	本土设计	local design

民族风格	traditional style	地域性	regionalism
现代功能空间	modern functional space	场所感	localization
信息化时代	the Information Age	立足之本	roots

Directions: Please summarize the passage in English. Your summary should be about 150—200 words. The word bank above may give you some help.

_____
_____
_____
_____
_____
_____
_____
_____

Passage B

Chicago School Architecture

Chicago's architecture is famous throughout the world and one style is referred to as the Chicago School. The style is also known as Commercial Style. In the history of architecture, the Chicago School was a school of architects active in Chicago at the turn of the 20th century. They were among the first to promote the new technologies of steel-frame construction in commercial buildings, and developed a spatial aesthetic which co-evolved with, and then came to influence, parallel developments in European Modernism. A "Second Chicago School" later emerged in the 1940s and 1970s which pioneered new building technologies and structural systems such as the tube-frame structure.

First Chicago School

While the term "Chicago School" is widely used to describe buildings in the city during the 1880s and 1890s, this term has been disputed by scholars, in particular in reaction to Carl Condit's 1952 book *The Chicago School of Architecture*. Historians such as H. Allen Brooks, Winston Weisman and Daniel Bluestone have pointed out that the phrase suggests a unified set of aesthetic or conceptual precepts, when, in fact, Chicago buildings of the era displayed a wide variety of styles and techniques. Contemporary publications used the phrase "Commercial Style" to describe the innovative tall buildings of the era rather than proposing any sort of unified "school."

Some of the distinguishing features of the Chicago School are the use of steel-frame buildings with masonry cladding (usually terra cotta), allowing large plate-glass window areas and limiting the amount of exterior ornamentation. Sometimes elements of neoclassical architecture are used in Chicago School skyscrapers. Many Chicago School skyscrapers contain the three parts of a classical column. The first floor functions as the base, the middle stories, usually with little ornamental detail, act as the shaft of the column, and the last floor or two, often capped with a cornice and often with more ornamental detail, represent the capital.

The "Chicago window" originated in this school. It is a three-part window consisting of a large fixed center panel flanked by two smaller double-hung sash windows. The arrangement of windows on the facade typically creates a grid pattern, with some projecting out from the facade forming bay windows. The Chicago window combined the functions of light-gathering and natural ventilation; a single central pane was usually fixed, while the two surrounding panes were operable. These windows were often deployed in bays, known as oriel windows, that projected out over the street.

Architects whose names are associated with the Chicago School include Henry Hobson Richardson, Dankmar Adler, Daniel Burnham, William Holabird, William LeBaron Jenney, Martin Roche, John Root, Solon S. Beman, and Louis Sullivan. Frank Lloyd Wright started in the firm of Adler and Sullivan but created his own Prairie Style of architecture.

The Home Insurance Building, which some regarded as the first skyscraper in the world, was built in Chicago in 1885 and was demolished in 1931. Some of the more famous Chicago School buildings include (in Chicago):

- Auditorium Building
- Sullivan Center
- Reliance Building
- Gage Group Buildings
- Chicago Building
- Brooks Building
- Fisher Building
- Heyworth Building
- Leiter I Building
- Leiter II Building
- Marquette Building
- Monadnock Building
- Montauk Building
- Rookery Building

Buildings outside Chicago include:

- Blount Building, Pensacola, Florida
- Wainwright Building, St. Louis, Missouri
- Nicholas Building, Melbourne, Australia
- Union Bank Building, Winnipeg, Manitoba, Canada
- Consultancy House, Dunedin, New Zealand
- Manchester Courts, Christchurch, New Zealand (demolished 2011)

Second Chicago School

In the 1940s, a "Second Chicago School" emerged from the work of Ludwig Mies van der Roh and his efforts of education at the Illinois Institute of Technology in Chicago. Its first and pure expression was the 860—880 Lake Shore Drive Apartments (1951) and their technologic achievements. This was supported and enlarged in the 1960s due to the ideas of structural engine Fazlur Khan. He introduced a new structural system of framed tubes in skyscraper design a construction. The Bangladeshi engineer Fazlur Khan defined the framed tube structure as "a three dimensional space structure composed of three, four, or possibly more frames, braced frames, or shear walls, joined at or near their edges to form a vertical tube-like structural system capable of resisting lateral forces in any direction by cantilevering from the foundation." Closely spaced interconnected exterior columns form the tube. Horizontal loads, for example wind, are supported by the structure as a whole. About half the exterior surface is available for windows. Framed tubes allow fewer interior columns, and so create more usable floor space. Where larger openings like garage doors are required, the tube frame must be interrupted, with transfer girders used to maintain structural integrity.

The first building to apply the tube-frame construction was the DeWitt-Chestnut Apartment Building which Khan designed and was completed in Chicago by 1963. This laid the foundations for the tube structures of many other later skyscrapers, including his own John Hancock Center and Willis Tower, and can be seen in the construction of the World Trade Center, Petronas Towers, Jin Mao Building, and most other super-tall skyscrapers since the 1960s.

Today, there are different styles of architecture all throughout the city, such as the Chicago School, neo-classical, art deco, modern, and postmodern.

(869 words)

1. The passage was retrieved and adapted from: http://en.wikipedia.org/wiki/Chicago_school_(architecture)

Directions: Please summarize the passage in Chinese. Your summary should be about 200—300 words.

___
___
___
___
___
___
___
___
___
___
___
___

Unit 5

LAW AND SOCIETY

But how is this legal plunder to be identified? Quite simply. See if the law takes from some persons what belongs to them, and gives it to other persons to whom it does not belong. See if the law benefits one citizen at the expense of another by doing what the citizen himself cannot do without committing a crime.

—By Frederic Bastiat

Learning Objectives

Upon completion of this unit, you should be able to:

Remember & Understand	★ recognize legal terms; ★ identify and explain in your own words the legal issues and the main points of Text A and Text B;
Analyze & Apply	★ learn to write sentences with parenthesis structure; ★ use corpora to learn the collocational patterns of a word; ★ make reference to the thesis and/or the major points of Text A and Text B in your writing;
Evaluate & Create	★ learn to write on organization chart; ★ participate in both sides of an interview process; ★ deliver a clear and coherent oral presentation of your views on the legal affairs.

Unit 5

Part One Lead-in

Section 1 Listening

Task 1 Filling in the Blanks

Directions: Please fill in the blanks with one or two words on the basis of what you have heard in the passage.

   The rule of law is a system of rules and rights that enables fair and functioning societies.

   We ____1____ this system ____2____ one in which the following four ____3____ principles are upheld:

- The government and its officials and ____4____ as well as individuals and private entities are ____5____ under the law.
- The laws are clear, ____6____, stable, and just; are applied ____7____; and protect fundamental rights, including the security of persons and ____8____.
- The process by which the laws are enacted, administered, and enforced is ____9____.
- Justice is delivered timely by competent, ethical, and ____10____ representatives and neutrals who are of sufficient number, have adequate resources, and ____11____ of the communities they serve.

Task 2 Group Discussion

Directions: Please discuss the following questions in pairs or groups based on what you have heard.

1. According to the talk, who are responsible for the law?
2. What's your own understanding of fundamental rights?
3. How can we secure the rule of law in a society?

Section 2 Watching

Task 1 Group Discussion

Directions: Please watch the video "The Rule of Law" and discuss the following question below in pairs or groups.

1. What is this video clip mainly about?
2. Whose points have been quoted to illustrate rule of law?
3. Why does the speaker say the law must protect individuals against complete state power?

Task 2 Reciting

Directions: Listen and try to imitate the speaker to recite the following points on rule of law.

   The rule of law is preferable to that of any individual. On the same principle, even if it be better for certain individuals to govern, they should be made only guardians and ministers of the law.

   Freedom of men under government, is, to have a standing rule to live by, common to every one of that society, and made by the legislative power erected in it; a liberty to follow my own will in all things...where the rule prescribes not; and not to be subject to the inconstant, uncertain, unknown, arbitrary will of another man.

Part Two Reading and Writing

Text A

Law and Society
Phil Harris

1   One of the many ways in which human societies can be *distinguished* from animal groups is by reference to social rules. We eat and sleep at certain *intervals*; we work on certain days for certain periods; our behavior towards others is controlled, directly and indirectly, through moral standards, religious *doctrines*, social traditions and legal rules. To take one specific example: we may be born with a "mating instinct", but it is through social rules that the attempt is made to channel this "instinct" into the most common socially-sanctioned form of relationship—*heterosexual* marriage. Marriage is only one example of social behavior being governed through rules. Legal rules are especially significant in the world of business, with matters such as banking, money, credit and employment all *regulated* to some extent through law. Indeed, in a complex society like our own, it is hard to find any area of activity which is completely *free from* legal control. Driving, working, being a parent, handling property—all these are touched in some way by law. Even a basic activity like eating is indirectly affected by law, *in that* the food we eat is required by legal rules to meet *rigorous* standards of purity, *hygiene* and even description.

2   Most of us, if asked to define law, would probably do so in terms of rules. A rule *prescribes* what activity may, should or should not be carried out, or refers to activities which should be carried out in a specific way. Rules of law may forbid certain activity—murder and theft are prohibited through rules of criminal law—or they may *impose* certain conditions under which activity may be carried out. Again the law contains some rules which we might call "power-*conferring*" rules: rules which enable certain activities to be carried out with some form of legal backing and protection. Because a rule guides us in what we may, ought or ought not to do, it is said to be *normative*. We can best grasp the meaning of this term if we contrast a normative statement, telling us what ought to happen, with a factual statement, which tells us what does happen. All rules, whether legal, moral or just *customary*, are normative, laying down standards of behavior to which we ought to conform if the rule affects us.

3   Another important aspect of rules in general, and legal rules in particular, is the phenomenon of obedience to those rules, and the acceptance that those rules are both *legitimate* and authoritative. There are many analyses of these issues, let us briefly consider one or two of them. For example, Austin's idea of why we obey law is found in his notion of the "habit of obedience" to the *sovereign* body in a society, which

together with the ever-present threat of sanctions, explains obedience to law. Few, however, would accept this idea as an adequate explanation. It is a questionable *assumption* that we obey law *out of* habit or for fear of official *reprisals*. Rather, as Hart argues, most of us *conform* to law because of more complex social and *psychological* processes. Hart's own explanation of obedience to law lies in the idea of some inner psychological *inclination* whereby we consider it "right and proper" to do so. Hart calls this acceptance the "internal" aspect of obedience to law, and argues that people usually obey because of such acceptance.

Of course, as Hart acknowledges, there are exceptions. Some might obey out of a genuine worry about the consequences of disobedience; others might disagree with the *entirety* of the legal and social arrangements in our society, but obey the law out of sheer convenience. Everything depends, of course, upon the kind of society and legal system *in question*, for an extreme and oppressive *regime* might deliberately obtain obedience to its dictates by *instilling* terror into the population. In our own society, however, few of us would seriously dispute the idea that most people accept the *legitimacy* of existing legal, social and political authority, as defined through constitutional doctrines and principles, and our everyday "common-sense" notions of legal authority.

This question of the idea of authority in society is worthy of closer attention, however. Max Weber, a sociologist, identified three types of authority in social groups. First, he argued, the authority of a leader or ruler may be the result of the personal, individual characteristics of that leader—his or her *charisma*—which *sets* that person *from* the rest. Examples might be Jesus, Napoleon, or Eva Peron in Argentina, or Winston Churchill in Britain, all of whom, it might be said, to some extent and to varying degrees, rose to their *exalted* positions and maintained those positions as leaders through their extraordinary strong personalities.

A second type of authority, according to Weber, is *traditional* authority, where obedience to the leader or regimes is sustained because it is traditional: "it has always been so." Third, Weber identifies in modern western societies a form of authority which he calls *rational*-legal or *bureaucratic*, where the authority of the regime is legitimized not through personal charismatic leadership, nor through pure tradition, but through rules and procedures. Weber's three types of authority have rarely, if ever, existed in reality in their pure form. Most societies have elements of more than one type. Our own society has elements of all three—the traditional (as seen in the ceremonies surrounding, say, the formal opening of Parliament), the charismatic (such as the leadership of Churchill during the Second World War) and the rational-legal (as in bureaucratic political and legal institutions such as the civil service).

(927 words)

New Words

distinguish	[dɪˈstɪŋgwɪʃ]	v.	to notice or understand the difference between two things, or to make one person or thing seem different from another 区分,分辨;使有所区别
interval	[ˈɪntəvəl]	n.	a period between two events or times, or the space between two points 间隔;间距
doctrine	[ˈdɒktrɪn]	n.	a belief or set of beliefs, esp. political or religious, taught and accepted by a particular group（尤指政治或宗教的）信条,教义,学说
heterosexual	[ˌhetərəʊˈseksjʊəl]	n.	a person who is sexually attracted to people of the opposite sex 异性恋者
regulate	[ˈregjʊleɪt]	v.	to control sth. esp. by making it work in a particular way（尤指使按照某种方式运作而）控制,管理;调节,调整
rigorous	[ˈrɪgərəs]	a.	careful to look at or consider every part of sth. to make certain it is correct or safe 严密的,缜密的,严谨的
hygiene	[ˈhaɪdʒiːn]	n.	the degree to which people keep themselves or their environment clean, esp. to prevent disease 卫生;卫生状况
prescribe	[prɪˈskraɪb]	v.	(of a doctor) to say what medical treatment someone should have（医生）开（药）,为……开（药）;嘱咐（疗法）
impose	[ɪmˈpəʊz]	v.	to officially force a rule, tax, punishment, etc. to be obeyed or received 推行;强制实行
confer	[kənˈfɜːr]	v.	to exchange ideas on a particular subject, often in order to reach a decision on what action to take（常指为达成行动决议而）商讨,商议,协商
normative	[ˈnɔːmətɪv]	a.	relating to rules, or making people obey rules, esp. rules of behavior 标准的,规范的
customary	[ˈkʌstəməri]	a.	usual 惯常的
legitimate	[ləˈdʒɪtɪmət]	a.	allowed by law 合法的,正当的,法律允许的
sovereign	[ˈsɒvərɪn]	a.	having the highest power or being completely independent 至高无上的;完全独立的
assumption	[əˈsʌmpʃən]	n.	sth. that you accept as true without question or proof 假定,假设;臆断
reprisal	[rɪˈpraɪzəl]	n.	(an example of) activity against another person, esp. as a punishment by military forces or a political group（尤指军事或政治的）报复,报复行动

Unit 5

conform	[kənˈfɔːm]	v.	to behave according to the usual standards of behaviour which are expected by a group or society 顺从,遵从;随大流,顺应习俗
psychological	[ˌsaɪkəlˈɒdʒɪkəl]	a.	relating to the human mind and feelings 心理的;心理学的
inclination	[ˌɪnklɪˈneɪʃən]	n.	a preference or tendency, or a feeling that makes a person want to do sth. 倾向;爱好;意向
entirety	[ɪnˈtaɪərɪti]	n.	with all parts included 整体,整个
regime	[reɪˈʒiːm]	n.	mainly disapproving a particular government or a system or method of government 政府;政权;政体 a particular way of operating or organizing a business 组织方法;管理体制;体系
instill	[ɪnˈstɪl]	v.	to put a feeling, idea or principle gradually into someone's mind, so that it has a strong influence on the way they think or behave 逐渐灌输
legitimacy	[ləˈdʒɪtɪməsi]	n.	the quality of being legal or acceptable 合法性;合理性
charisma	[kəˈrɪzmə]	n.	a special power which some people have naturally which makes them able to influence other people and attract their attention and admiration 超凡的个人魅力;吸引力;超凡气质
exalt	[ɪɡˈzɒlt]	v.	[formal] to raise someone to a higher rank or more powerful position 晋升,提拔 [old] to praise someone a lot 颂扬,高度赞扬
rational	[ˈræʃənəl]	a.	showing clear thought or reason 头脑清醒的,理智的
bureaucratic	[ˌbjʊərəˈkrætɪk]	a.	relating to a system of controlling or managing a country, company or organization that is operated by a large number of officials 官僚政治的,官僚主义的

Phrases & Expressions

free from	not affected by sth. harmful or unpleasant 不受……伤害(或影响)的
in that	because 因为,由于
out of	because of 因为
(sb. or sth.) in question	the thing or person that is being discussed 讨论中的
set sb./sth. from	make sb./sth. different from or better than others 使……与众不同;使……优于

 **Notes**

1. The text was adapted from a popular textbook *An Introduction to Law* by Phil Harris. Since the publication of its first edition, the book has become the definitive student introduction to the subject. The author places emphasis on an understanding of the law and the legal system as living institutions within society, deals with how appreciation of the rules and legal structures both reflect and influence changes in social, economic and political life and gives a clear understanding of fundamental legal concepts and their importance within society.
2. Phil Harris is now Emeritus Professor of Legal Education at Sheffield Hallam University. Head of Law subject group in 1980s, and again in 1990s. Responsible for developing the full-time law degree in mid-80s. Actively researched in the field of legal education, producing and publishing three reports of surveys into UK legal education.

Task 1   Generating the Outline

Directions: Please identify the thesis of the passage and the main point of each paragraph and find out how these points develop the thesis. You may use the table below to help you.

The thesis:	Social rules are significant for human societies and people may _____ out of different consideration.
Para. 1: *The differentiation:*	Human societies differ from animal groups in _____.
Para. 2: *The definition:*	Law is about rules that set _____ which people must conform to.
Para. 3: *The analysis:*	Austin believes that people obey law out of _____. Hart's acceptance theory has _____ inclination.
Para. 4: *The exceptions:*	People might obey law because of _____ about certain consequence of disobedience or _____.
Paras. 5—6: *The elaboration:*	Max Weber identifies three types of authority, namely, _____ _____.

Task 2   Understanding the Text

Directions: Please answer the following questions.

1. What's your understanding of the relationship between law and society?
2. What does it mean by "mating instinct"? (Para.1)
3. In what way does marriage differ from "mating instinct"? (Para.1)
4. Why does the author say even eating is affected by law? Please cite a few examples from dail life to illustrate. (Para.1)
5. Why are rules normative? (Para. 2)
6. Is Austin's notion of the "habit of obedience" to the sovereign body popular among people

Why? (Para. 3)
7. How does Hart explain people's conforming to law? (Para. 3)
8. Can you give a few examples of oppressive regime that seek obedience through terror in history? (Para. 4)
9. What does Max Weber mean by bureaucratic authority?(Para. 6)
10. Do you agree with Max Weber's categorization of authority in social groups? And why or why not? (Paras. 5—6)

Task 3 Vocabulary Building

Directions: Compare and contrast the five most frequent collocational patterns of the following words in different corpora or different parts of the same corpus. And then discuss the implications of the results.

> behavior   instinct   regulate   govern   criminal

adj. + moral

word (%)	public	good	true	good	high	loose
sino	22.27	9.67	0.88	9.67	3.22	0
bnc	3.02	0.34	0.50	0.34	0.50	0.84

v. + moral

word (%)	improve	have	get	offend	follow	corrupt
sino	10.55	7.91	0.29	0	3.22	1.17
bnc	0	2.35	1.01	0.50	0	0

(来源: 句酷批改网句料库字典之"英国英语综合"部分, www.pigai.org)

Task 4 Learning the Phrases

Directions: Please fill in the blanks in the sentences below with the phrases listed in the box. Change the forms if necessary. Notice that some phrases need to be used more than once.

> to some extent   in that   instill into
> in particular   at intervals   distinguish from

1. They tried to _____ such new ideas _____ students' minds.
2. I am interested in stories in general, and in detective stories _____.
3. There is something about music that _____ it _____ all other art forms.
4. She woke him for his medicines _____ throughout the night.
5. A shopping mall would _____ a spirit of modernity _____ this village.
6. Criticism and self-criticism is necessary _____ it helps us to correct our mistakes.
7. However, the evidence is thin and, _____, ambiguous.
8. Human beings are superior to animals _____ they can use language as a tool of communication.

9. Several red and white barriers marked the road _____ of about a mile.
10. All mothers share _____ in the tension of a wedding.

Task 5 Studying the Sentence Structure
Sentences with Parenthesis Structure
Sentences from the text
1. Most of us, if asked to define law, would probably do so in terms of rules. (Para. 2)
2. All rules, whether legal, moral or just customary, are normative, laying down standards of behavior to which we ought to conform if the rule affects us. (Para. 2)

Directions: Please follow the examples and use parenthesis to combine two sentences into one.
Tips

> 1. Parenthesis is an explanatory, qualifying, or appositive word, phrase, clause, or sentence that interrupts a syntactic construction without otherwise affecting it.
> 2. It could be left out and still form grammatically correct text.
> 3. Parentheses are usually marked off by round or square brackets, dashes, or commas.

1. Liftshare is a car-sharing website.
   Liftshare boasts around 400,000 members, up from under 200,000 in 2003.
   _____
   _____

2. GE is an American engineering conglomerates.
   General Electric (GE), is now putting one through its paces.
   _____
   _____

3. People in Tokyo have taken Eataly to their hearts and wallets.
   They did this after a slow start.
   _____
   _____

Task 6 Paraphrasing Difficult Sentences
1. One of the many ways in which human societies can be distinguished from animal groups is by reference to social rules.
   _____
   _____

2. Indeed, in a complex society like our own, it is hard to find any area of activity which is completely free from legal control.
   _____
   _____

3. Another important aspect of rules in general, and legal rules in particular, is the phenomenon of obedience to those rules, and the acceptance that those rules are both legitimate and authoritative.

4. It is a questionable assumption that we obey law out of habit or for fear of official reprisals.

5. Some might obey out of a genuine worry about the consequences of disobedience; others might disagree with the entirety of the legal and social arrangements in our society, but obey the law out of sheer convenience.

Task 7   Summarizing the Text

Directions: Please summarize Text A in 120 words. You may use the table in Task 1 to help you.

Task 8   Writing with Organization Charts

Directions: Study the following organization chart and write a passage about the agency department system with about 100—150 words.

Tips

1. A chart often enables one to visualize an organization, by means of the picture it presents.
2. It is also used to show the relation of one department to another, or others, or of one function of an organization to another, or others.
3. The organization chart is a diagram showing graphically the relation of one official to another, or others, of a company or organization.

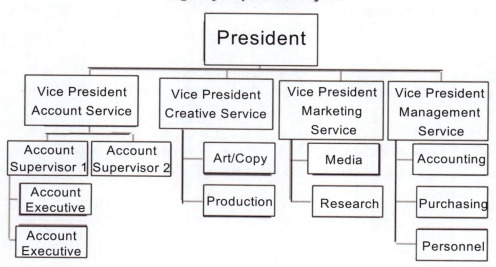

Part Three Reading and Speaking

Text B

The Function of Law
Raymond Wacks

Order

1   Football, chess, bridge are unthinkable without rules. A casual poker club could not *function* without rules by which its members are expected to abide. It is not surprising therefore that when they are formed into larger social groups, humans have always required laws. Without law, society is barely *conceivable*. We tend, unfortunately, towards *egoism*. The restraint that law imposes on our liberty is the price we pay for living in a community. "We are slaves of the law," wrote the great Roman lawyer Cicero, "so that we may be free." And the law has provided the security and self-determination that has, in large part, *facilitated* social and political advancement.

2   The cliché "law and order" is perhaps more accurately *rendered* "law for order." Without law, it is widely assumed, order would be *unattainable*. And order—or what is now popularly called "security"—is the central aim of most governments. It is an essential *prerequisite* of a society that aspires to safeguard the well-being of its members.

3   Thomas Hobbes famously declared that in his natural state—prior to the social

contract—the condition of man was "*solitary*, poor, nasty, brutish and short." Law and government are required, Hobbes argues, if we are to *preserve* order and security. We therefore need, by the social contract, to surrender our natural freedom in order to create an orderly society. His philosophy is nowadays regarded as somewhat *authoritarian*, placing order over justice.

He recognizes that we are fundamentally equal, mentally and physically: even the weakest has the strength to kill the strongest. This equality, he suggests, *engenders* discord. We tend to quarrel, he argues, for three main reasons: competition (for limited supplies of material possessions), distrust, and glory (we remain *hostile* in order to preserve our powerful reputations). As a consequence of our inclination toward conflict, Hobbes concludes that we are in a natural state of continuous war of all against all, where no moral exist, and all live in *perpetual* fear. Until this state of war ceases, all have a right to everything, including another person's life. Order is, of course, only part of the functions of law story.

Justice

Though the law unquestionably protects order, it has another vital purpose. In the words of the 20th-century English judge Lord Denning: The law as I see it has two great objects: to preserve order and to do justice; and the two do not always *coincide*. Those whose training lies toward order, put certainty before justice; whereas those training lies towards the redress of *grievances*, put justice before certainty. The right solution lies in keeping the proper balance between the two.

The pursuit of justice must lie at the heart of any legal system. The virtual equation of law with justice has a long history. It is to be found in the writing of the Greek philosophers, in the Bible, in the Roman Emperor Justinian's *codification* of the law. The quest for clarity in the analysis of the concept of justice has, however, not been unproblematic. Both Plato and Aristotle sought to illuminate its *principal* features. Indeed, Aristotle's approach remains the launching pad for most discussions of justice. He argues that justice *consists in* treating equals equally and unequals unequally, *in proportion to* their inequality.

Acknowledging that the equality implied in justice could either be *arithmetical* (based on the identity of the persons concerned) or *geometrical* (based on maintaining the same proportion), Aristotle distinguishes between corrective justice, on the one hand, and *distributive* justice, on the other. The former is the justice of the courts which is applied in the redress of crimes or civil wrongs. It requires that all men are to be treated equally. The latter (distributive justice), he argues, concerns giving each according to his desert or merit. This, in Aristotle's views, is principally the concern of the legislator.

In his *celebrated* book, *The Concept of Law*, H.L.A. Hart contends that in the modern world the principle that human beings *are entitled to* be treated alike had become so well established that racial discrimination is usually defended on the ground that those discriminated against are not "fully human."

9 There are *numerous* competing approaches to the meaning of justice, including those that echo Hobbes' social contract. A modern version is to be found in the important writings of John Rawls who advances the idea of justice as fairness which seeks to *arrive at* objective principles of justice that would *hypothetically* be agreed upon by individuals who, under a veil of ignorance, do not know to which sex, class, religion, or social position they belong. Each person represents a social class, but they have no ideas whether they are clever or dim, strong or weak. Nor do they know in which country or in what period they are living, they possess only certain elementary knowledge about the laws of science and psychology. In this state of *blissful* ignorance, they must *unanimously* decide upon a contract the general principles of which will define the terms under which they will live as a society. And in doing so, they are moved by rational self-interest: each individual seeks those principles which will give him or her the best chance of attaining his or her chosen *conception* of the good life, whatever that happens to be.

(886 words)

New Words

function	[ˈfʌŋkʃən]	v.	to work or operate 运转；工作；起作用
conceivable	[kənˈsiːvəbl]	a.	possible to imagine or to believe 可想象的；可以相信的
egoism	[ˈegəʊɪzəm]	n.	thinking only about yourself and considering yourself better and more important than other people 自大，自负
facilitate	[fəˈsɪlɪˌteɪt]	v.	to make possible or easier 促进，使便利
render	[ˈrendə]	v.	to change words into a different language or form 翻译
unattainable	[ˌʌnəˈteɪnəbl]	a.	not able to be achieved 无法实现的
prerequisite	[priːˈrekwɪzɪt]	n.	sth. which must exist or happen before sth. else can exist or happen 先决条件；前提
solitary	[ˈsɒlətri]	a.	a solitary person or thing is the only person or thing in a place 独自的，唯一的，单个的
preserve	[prɪˈzɜːv]	v.	to keep sth. as it is, especially in order to prevent it from decaying or being damaged or destroyed; to conserve 保护，维护；保留
authoritarian	[əˌθɔːrəˈteriən]	a.	demanding that people totally obey and refusing to allow them freedom to act as they wish 独裁的，专制的
engender	[enˈdʒendə]	v.	to make people have a particular feeling or make situation start to exist 引起（某种感觉），导致

Unit 5

hostile	[ˈhɑ:stl]	a.	unfriendly and not liking or agreeing with sth. 不友好的,敌对的
perpetual	[pəˈpetʃuəl]	a.	continuing forever in the same way 永久的,长期的
coincide	[ˌkəʊɪnˈsaɪd]	v.	to happen at or near the same time (几乎)同时发生
grievance	[ˈgri:vəns]	n.	a complaint or a strong feeling that you have been treated unfairly 不平,委屈,抱怨,牢骚
codification	[ˌkəʊdɪfɪˈkeɪʃn]	n.	the act of arranging sth., such as laws or rules, into a system 法典编成,(法典、条例等)编纂
principal	[ˈprɪnsəpəl]	a.	first in order of importance 最重要的
arithmetical	[ˌærɪθˈmetɪkl]	a.	involving adding and multiplying, etc. of numbers 算术的
geometrical	[dʒɪəˈmetrɪkl]	a.	describes a pattern or arrangement that is made up of shapes such as squares, triangles or rectangles 几何图形的,几何的
distributive	[dɪˈstrɪbjʊtɪv]	a.	(of a mathematical operation) giving the same result whether parts are acted on in combination or separately 分布的;分配的,分发的
celebrated	[ˈseləˌbreɪtɪd]	a.	famous for some special quality or ability 著名的,驰名的
numerous	[ˈnu:mərəs]	a.	many 许多的,大量的
hypothetically	[ˌhaɪpəˈθetɪklɪ]	ad.	imagined or suggested but not necessarily real or true 假定地,假设地
blissful	[ˈblɪsfl]	a.	extremely or completely happy 极乐的,极幸福的
unanimously	[jʊˈnænəməslɪ]	ad.	if a group of people are unanimous, they all agree about one particular matter or vote the same way, and if a decision or judgment is unanimous, it is formed or supported by everyone in a group (团体)意见一致的;(决定或裁决)一致通过的,获得全体支持的
conception	[kənˈsepʃən]	n.	an idea of what sth. or someone is like, or a basic understanding of a situation or a principle 观念,概念,见解;构想

Phrases & Expressions

consist in	to have sth. as a main and necessary part or quality 在于,存在于
proportion to	used to say that two things are connected, so that an increase in one is directly related to an increase in the other 与某物成比例

be entitled to	be given someone the right to do or have sth. 被给予……的权利；符合资格
arrive at	to reach an agreement about sth. 达成……；做出……；得出……

1. *Law: A Very Short Introduction* is a clear, jargon-free book that introduces the essentials of law and legal systems in a lively, accessible, and stimulating manner. Explaining the main concepts, terms, and processes of the legal system, it focuses on the Western tradition (the common law and the civil law), but also includes discussions of other legal systems, such as customary law and Islamic law. And it looks to the future too, as globalization and rapid advances in technology place increasing strain on our current legal system.

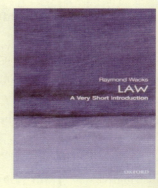

2. Raymond Wacks is Emeritus Professor of Law and Legal Theory at the University of Hong Kong. His books include *Understanding Jurisprudence: An Introduction to Legal Theory* (OUP, 2005); and *Philosophy of Law: A Very Short Introduction* (OUP, 2006). He has appeared on BBC television, and CNN and BBC radio, and has written for publications such as *The Times* (London), *New Statesman*, and *The Spectator*.

Task 1　Summarizing

Directions: Read Text B and complete the following paragraph based on your understanding of the text.

　　In a poker club all members must abide by certain _____ so as to sustain their activities. In the same sense, _____ is essential for a social group to run smoothly. In some way, we may have to sacrifice our _____ so as to live in a social group. According to Thomas Hobbes, _____ and _____ are necessary provided we are to maintain an orderly society. He argues that _____, _____, _____ are the main sources of discord. As far as justice is concerned, Denning believed the law aims to _____ and _____. Prolific literature on law in history illustrates that the quest for justice is the core of any _____. However, people's approach to the meaning of justice varied greatly. Aristotle distinguishes between _____ and _____. John Rawls studies justice from the perspective of _____. However, he contends that individuals are ignorant of their own _____.

Task 2　Synthesizing Information

Directions: Based on what you have learned from rule of law in the video clip and Text A, you may interview five of your classmates about their unhappy experiences of being re-checked at the gates of supermarkets. Your interview should contain no fewer than five questions. Plan your interview

questions carefully so that you can get a deep understanding of the issue whether it is a serious legal affair and how to treat this legally. Take notes of the answers you get from each of your interviewees. You may use the following tables to note down the keywords of your interview questions and the keywords of the answers you collect.

Table 1 Keywords for interview questions

1.	
2.	
3.	
4.	
5.	
6.	
7.	
8.	
9.	
10.	

Table 2

	Positive answers	Negative answers
Finding 1		
reasons		
Finding 2		
reasons		
Finding 3		
reasons		

Task 3 Making Comments

Justice delayed is justice denied. This is a legal maxim meaning that if legal redress is available for a party that has suffered some injury, but is not forthcoming in a timely fashion, it is effectively the same as having no redress at all. William Penn ever remarked almost the same— to delay justice is injustice. This principle is the basis for the right to a speedy trial and similar rights which are meant to speed up the legal system, because it is unfair for the injured party to have to sustain the injury with little hope for resolution. What do you think of the topic— to delay justice is injustice? Please illustrate your point.

Part Four Cross Cultural Communication

Passage A

权力的兽性

安立志

笼子多与动物有关,主要有两种功能,一是防止动物走失,二是防止动物伤人。

"把权力关进制度的笼子里",概因为权力具有虎狼之兽性。

在政治发展史上,中外学者都意识到"国家权力从来就是一种危险的、却又是必要的恶"。从而提出如何理性地对待权力的多重性质。

西方学者从自然人到政治人,特别是对由权力勾引出的隐藏在人性深处的兽性,做出了深刻分析。古希腊哲学家亚里士多德在两千多年前就说过:"人类由于志趣善良而有所成就,成为最优良的动物;如果不讲礼法、违背正义,他就堕落为最恶劣的动物。""让一个个人来统治,这就在政治中混入了兽性的因素。"国家无疑是权力的集合体。17世纪英国哲学家托马斯·霍布斯这样认为:"号称'国民的整体'或'国家'的这个庞然大物'利维坦',是用艺术造成的,它只是一个'人造的人'。"而这个"利维坦",在《圣经》中则是象征邪恶的海怪,也是基督教中恶魔的代名词。

……

在我国古代,孔子亦有"苛政猛于虎"的论述——这一思想在两千年后被英国思想家罗素所借用,将之翻译为"暴虐的政治比虎还凶",并作为其名著《权力论》"节制权力"一章的主题。所以孔子历来主张"王道"与"仁政"。韩非子作为法家的集大成者,也曾系统论述过政治场域中的法、术、势。在韩非子眼里,势作为权力的外在张力,显然具有兽性的一面,"势者,养虎狼之心,而成暴乱之事者也,此天下之大患也"。

权力的兽性,通常有两个特征,一是贪婪,二是残忍。非洲大草原上的狮子,其捕食猎物固然贪婪与残忍,却是其维持种群生存与繁衍之必需。正如伯特兰·罗素所指出,"动物只要能够生存和生殖就感到满足。"而"人类的某些欲望跟动物的欲望不同,是根本无止境的,是不能得到完全满足的"。

……

习近平总书记要求"把权力关进制度的笼子里",具有明确的针对性与紧迫的现实性。落实总书记的要求,决不能仅仅变成会议官话与文件套话,而应针对现存的制度缺陷与制度漏洞进行调整与完善,建立行之有效的制衡和监督体系,真正把权力这只野兽关进制度的笼子里。

(821 word)

Unit 5

注解

1. 本文节选改编自安立志发表于《南方日报》的文章《权力的兽性》，国内多家报刊、杂志网站转载。
2. 作者安立志，山东杂文作家，杂文作品见于境内外百余家报刊。

Word Bank

笼子	cage	正义	justice
专制	dictatorship	监管	supervision

Directions: Please summarize the passage in English. Your summary should be about 150—200 words.

Passage B

None of us are doing what we think is right. Why not? We don't trust the law because it gives us the worst of both worlds: It's random—anybody can sue for almost anything and take it to a jury, not even an effort at consistency—and it's also too detailed. In the areas that are regulated, there are so many rules which no human could possibly know. Well how do you fix it? We could spend 10,000 lifetimes trying to prune this legal jungle. But the challenge here is not one of just amending the law, because the hurdle for success is trust.

Law is the platform for freedom, and people have to trust it. Trust is an essential condition to a free society. Life is complicated enough without legal fear. But law is different from other kinds of uncertainties, because it carries with it the power of state. And so the state can come in. It actually changes the way people think. It's like having a little lawyer on your shoulders all day long, whispering in your ear, "Could that go wrong? Might that go wrong?" It drives people from the smart part of the brain—that dark, deep well of the subconscious, where instincts and experience, and all the other factors of creativity and good judgment are—it drives us to the thin veneer of conscious logic.

Pretty soon the doctor's saying, "Well, I doubt if that headache could be a tumor, but who would protect me if it were? So maybe I'll just order the MRI." Then you've wasted 200 billion dollars in unnecessary tests. If you make people self-conscious about their judgments, studies show you will make them make worse judgments. If you tell the pianist to think about how she's hitting the notes when she's playing the piece, she can't play the piece. Self-consciousness is the enemy of accomplishment. Edison stated it best. He said, "Hell, we aren't got no rules around here, we're trying to accomplish something."

So, how do you restore trust? Tweaking the law's clearly not good enough, and tort reform, which is a great idea, lowers your cost if you're a businessperson, but it's like a Band-Aid on this gaping wound of distrust. States with extensive tort reform still suffer all these pathologies. So, what's needed is not just to limit claims, but actually create a dry ground of freedom. It turns out that freedom actually has a formal structure. And it is this: Law sets boundaries, and on one side of those boundaries are all the things you can't do or must do—you can't steal, you've got to pay your taxes—but those same boundaries are supposed to define and protect a dry ground of freedom. What's needed now is to rebuild these boundaries. And it's especially important to rebuild them for lawsuits. Because what people can sue for establishes the boundaries for everybody else's freedom. If someone brings a lawsuit over, "A kid fell off the seesaw," it doesn't matter what happens in the lawsuit, all the seesaws will disappear. No one will want to take the risk of a lawsuit. And that's what's happened. There are no seesaws, jungle gyms, merry-go-rounds, climbing ropes, nothing that would interest a kid over the age of four, because there's no risk associated with it.

Life is too complex for a software program. All these choices involve value judgments and social norms, not objective facts. This is what we have, the philosophy we have to change to. And there are two essential elements of it: we have to simplify the law; we have to migrate from all this complexity towards general principles and goals. The constitution is only 16 pages long. It worked pretty well for 200 years.

Law has to be simple enough so that people can internalize it in their daily choices. If they can't internalize it, they won't trust it. And how do you make it simple? Because life is complex, and here is the hardest and biggest change: We have to restore the authority to judges and officials to interpret and apply the law. We have to rehumanize the law. To make law simple so that you feel free, the people in charge have to be free to use their judgment to interpret and apply the law in accord with reasonable social norms. As you're going down, and walking down the sidewalk during the day, you have to think that if there is a dispute, there's somebody in society who sees it as their job to affirmatively protect you if you're acting reasonably. That person doesn't exist today.

This is the hardest hurdle. It's actually not very hard. Ninety-eight percent of cases, this is a piece of cake. Maybe you've got a claim in small claims court for your lost pair of pants for $100, but not in a court of general jurisdiction for millions of dollars. Case dismissed without prejudice or refiling in small claims court.

But it's a hard hurdle because we got into this legal quicks and because we woke up in the 1960s to all these really bad values: racism, gender discrimination, pollution—they were bad values. And we wanted to create a legal system where no one could have bad values anymore. The problem is, we created a system where we eliminated the right to have good values. It doesn't mean that people in authority can do whatever they want. They're still bounded by legal goals and principles. The teacher is accountable to the principal, the judge is accountable to an appellate court, the president is accountable to voters. But the accountability's up the line judging the decision against the effect on everybody, not just on the disgruntled person. You can't run a society by the lowest common denominator.

We've been taught that authority is the enemy of freedom. It's not true. Authority, in fact, is essential to freedom. Law is a human institution; responsibility is a human institution. If teachers don't have authority to run the classroom, to maintain order, everybody who is learning suffers. If the judge doesn't have the authority to toss out unreasonable claims, then all of us go through the day looking over our shoulders. If the environmental agency can't decide that the power lines are good for the environment, then there's no way to bring the power from the wind farms to the city. A free society requires red lights and green lights, otherwise it soon descends into gridlock. That's what's happened to America.

What the world needs now is to restore the authority to make common choices. It's the only way to get our freedom back, and it's the only way to release the energy and passion needed so that we can meet the challenges of our time.

(1140 words)

Directions: Please summarize the passage in Chinese. Your summary should be about 200—300 words.

Unit 6

DEMAND, PRICE AND WEALTH

The Determinants of Demand

The relationship between price and quantity demanded is the starting point for building a model of consumer behaviour. Measuring the relationship between price and quantity demanded provides information which is used to create a demand schedule, from which a demand curve can be derived. Once a demand curve has been created, other determinants can be added to the model.

—From Economics Online Ltd.

Learning Objectives

Upon completion of this unit, you should be able to:

Remember & Understand	★ summarize the factors that may affect price; ★ identify and explain in your own words the thesis and the major points of Text A and Text B;
Analyze & Apply	★ make reference to the thesis and the major points of Text A and Text B in your writing or speaking; ★ produce sentences with predicative clauses or appositives; ★ use sentences or clauses with parallel structure or alliteration for rhetoric effect;
Evaluate & Create	★ be aware of the logic in your writing; ★ synthesize information between some related sources about the factors that may affect price; ★ deliver a clear and coherent oral presentation of your views on consumer demand and prices of commodities.

Unit 6

Part One Lead-in

Section 1 Listening

Task 1   Predicting

Directions: Get familiar with the following proper names and make some predictions about the listening material.

> the United Nations World Food Program 联合国世界粮食计划署
> the United States Agriculture Department 美国农业部
> the U.N. Environment Program 联合国环境规划署
> the United States Commodity Futures Trading Commission 美国商品期货交易委员会
> the Associated Press (AP) 美国联合通讯社

Could you predict what the listening material is about?

Task 2   Filling in the Blanks

Directions: Listen to a VOA economic report and find out the causes of the price rise of rice. Write your answers on the lines.

> **Reasons Behind the Price Rise of Rice**
> (a) _____ have played a part.
> (b) Nathan Childs says it is due to _____, but he thinks the main reason is _____.
> (c) The head of the U.N. Environment Program blames_____ for the high food prices.
> (d) Bart Chilton blamed _____ and _____.

Task 3   Reflecting

Directions: Please answer the following questions based on the listening material and your world knowledge.

1. What are the possible reasons that may cause the price rise of rice in China?
2. What are the positive and negative effects of the price rise of rice?
3. How should we guarantee that all people in China have enough food to eat?

Section 2 Watching

Task 1   Group Discussion

Directions: Please watch the video "Global Wealth Inequality" and discuss the three questions below in pairs or groups.

1. How does the speaker arrive at the conclusion that the global wealth is distributed unequally?
2. According to the speaker, why is global wealth inequality becoming worse? What's your view?
3. What do you think are the consequences of global wealth inequality?

Task 2 Finding out Figures as Supporting Evidence

Directions: Watch the video again and write down on the lines what the figures stand for. Then speak out the figures loudly.

80% of the world people _____
the richest 2% _____
7 billion _____
roughly 223 trillion dollars _____
43% of the world's wealth _____
the richest 300 v.s. the poorest 3 billion _____
3 times, 35 times, 80 times _____
about 130 billion dollars per year _____
more than 900 billion dollars per year _____
about 600 billion dollars per year _____

Part Two   Reading and Writing

Text A

Gradations of Consumers' Demand
Alfred Marshall

1   When a trader or a *manufacturer* buys anything to be used in production, or be sold again, his demand is based on his *anticipations* of the profits which he can *derive from* it. These profits depend at any time on *speculative* risks and on other causes, which will need to be considered later on. But in the long run the price which a trader or manufacturer can afford to pay for a thing depends on the prices which consumers will pay for it, or for the things made by aid of it. The *ultimate regulator* of all demands is therefore consumers' demand. And it is with that almost *exclusively* that we shall be concerned in the present Book.

2   *Utility* is taken to be *correlative* to Desire or Want. It has been already argued that desires cannot be measured directly, but only indirectly by the outward phenomena *to* which they give rise: and that in those cases with which economics is chiefly concerned the measure is found in the price which a person is willing to pay for the *fulfilment* or satisfaction of his desire. He may have desires and *aspirations* which are not consciously set for any satisfaction: but for the present we are concerned chiefly with those which do so aim; and we *assume* that the resulting satisfaction *corresponds* in general fairly well *to* that which was anticipated when the *purchase* was made.

3   There is an endless variety of wants, but there is a limit to each separate want.

This familiar and *fundamental tendency* of human nature may be stated in the law of satiable（可满足的）wants or of *diminishing* utility thus: The total utility of a thing to anyone (that is, the total pleasure or other benefit it *yields* him) increases with every increase in his stock of it, but not as fast as his stock increases. If his stock of it increases at a uniform rate the benefit derived from it increases at a diminishing rate. In other words, the additional benefit which a person derives from a given increase of his stock of a thing, diminishes with every increase in the stock that he already has.

That part of the thing which he is only just *induced* to purchase may be called his marginal purchase, because he is on the *margin* of doubt whether it is worth his while to *incur* the outlay（花费）required to obtain it. And the utility of his marginal purchase may be called the marginal utility of the thing to him. Or, if instead of buying it, he makes the thing himself, then its marginal utility is the utility of that part which he thinks it only just worth his while to make. And thus the law just given may be worded:

The marginal utility of a thing to anyone diminishes with every increase in the amount of it he already has.

There is however an *implicit* condition in this law which should be made clear. It is that we do not suppose time to be allowed for any *alteration* in the character or tastes of the man himself. It is therefore no exception to the law that the more good music a man hears, the stronger is his taste for it likely to become; that avarice（贪婪）and ambition are often insatiable; or that the *virtue* of cleanliness and the *vice* of drunkenness alike grow on what they *feed upon*. For in such cases our *observations range* over some period of time; and the man is not the same at the beginning as at the end of it. If we take a man as he is, without allowing time for any change in his character, the marginal utility of a thing to him diminishes steadily with every increase in his supply of it.

Now let us translate this law of diminishing utility into terms of price. Let us take an *illustration* from the case of a *commodity* such as tea, which is in *constant* demand and which can be purchased in small quantities. Suppose, for instance, that tea of a certain quality is to be had at 2s. per lb. A person might be willing to give 10s. for a single pound once a year rather than go without it altogether; while if he could have any amount of it for nothing he would perhaps not care to use more than 30 lbs. in the year. But as it is, he buys perhaps 10 lbs. in the year; that is to say, the difference between the satisfaction which he gets from buying 9 lbs. and 10 lbs. is enough for him to be willing to pay 2s. for it.

While the fact that he does not buy an eleventh pound, shows that he does not think that it would be worth an extra 2s. to him. That is, 2s. a pound measures the utility to him of the tea which lies at the margin or *terminus* or end of his purchases; it measures the marginal utility to him. If the price which he is just willing to pay for any pound be called his demand price, then 2s. is his marginal demand price. And our law may be worded:

9 The larger the amount of a thing that a person has the less, other things being equal (i.e. the purchasing power of money, and the amount of money at his command being equal), will be the price which he will pay for a little more of it, or in other words his marginal demand price for it diminishes.

(924 words)

New Words

gradation	[grəˈdeɪʃn]	n.	a series of systematic stages 等级
manufacturer	[ˌmænjʊˈfæktʃərə]	n.	a person or business that makes goods or owns a factory 厂商
anticipation	[ænˌtɪsɪˈpeɪʃn]	n.	expectation or hope 期待,希望;预期,预测
derive	[dɪˈraɪv]	v.	to receive or obtain from a source or origin 源于,来自
speculative	[ˈspekjʊlətɪv]	a.	engaging in business transactions involving considerable risk but offering the chance of large gains, esp. trading in commodities, stocks, etc., in the hope of profit from changes in the market price 投机的
ultimate	[ˈʌltɪmət]	a.	last; furthest or farthest; ending a process or series 最后的
regulator	[ˈregjʊleɪtə]	n.	a thing that controls or directs others by a rule 调节器
exclusively	[ɪkˈsklu:sɪvli]	ad.	only, merely 唯一地;专门地
utility	[ju:ˈtɪləti]	n.	the capacity of a commodity or a service to satisfy some human want 功用,效用
correlative	[kəˈrelətɪv]	a.	mutually related 相关的,关联的
fulfillment	[fʊlˈfɪlmənt]	n.	satisfaction 满足(感)
aspiration	[ˌæspəˈreɪʃn]	n.	strong desire, longing, or aim; ambition 强烈的愿望
assume	[əˈsju:m]	v.	to take for granted or without proof 假定,认为
purchase	[ˈpɜ:tʃəs]	n.	acquisition by the payment of money or its equivalent 购买;购买行为
fundamental	[ˌfʌndəˈmentl]	a.	serving as, or being an essential part of, a foundation or basis; basic; underlying 基本的,根本的
tendency	[ˈtendənsi]	n.	an inclination, bent, or predisposition to sth. 倾向,趋势
diminish	[dɪˈmɪnɪʃ]	v.	to make or cause to seem smaller, less, less important, reduce (使)减少,缩小;减弱
yield	[ji:ld]	v.	to give forth or produce 生产
induce	[ɪnˈdju:s]	v.	to lead or move by persuasion or influence, as to some action or state of mind 引诱;引起
margin	[ˈmɑ:dʒɪn]	n.	the point at which the return from economic activity barely covers the cost of production, and below which

Unit 6

			production is unprofitable 利润，盈余
incur	[ɪnˈkɜː]	v.	to come into or acquire (some consequence, usu. undesirable or injurious) 招致，引起；遭受
implicit	[ɪmˈplɪsɪt]	a.	implied, rather than expressly stated 不言明[含蓄]的
alteration	[ˌɔːltəˈreɪʃn]	n.	a change; modification or adjustment 变化，调整
virtue	[ˈvɜːtʃuː]	n.	moral excellence; goodness; righteousness 美德；德行；价值；长处
vice	[vaɪs]	n.	an immoral or evil habit or practice 恶习；不道德行为
observation	[ˌɒbzəˈveɪʃn]	n.	an act or instance of viewing or noting a fact or occurrence for some scientific or other special purpose 观察
range	[reɪndʒ]	v.	to stretch out or extend in a line, as things 延伸
illustration	[ˌɪləˈstreɪʃn]	n.	a comparison or an example intended for explanation 说明；例证
commodity	[kəˈmɒdəti]	n.	an article of trade or commerce, especially a product as distinguished from a service 商品
constant	[ˈkɒnstənt]	a.	not changing or varying; uniform; regular; invariable 不变的
terminus	[ˈtɜːmɪnəs]	n.	the end or extremity of anything 终点

Phrases & Expressions

derive from	to receive or obtain from a source or origin 源自
in the long run	in the course of long experience; in the end 从长远看
give rise to	to originate; produce; cause 引起
correspond to	to conform, be in agreement, or be consistent or compatible (with) 与……相应
feed upon	take sth. as food 以……为食

Notes

1. The text is excerpted from *Principles of Economics*, *Book III: On Wants and Their Satisfaction*. *Principles of Economics* was a leading political economy or economics textbook by Alfred Marshall, first published in 1890. It ran into many editions and was the standard text for generations of economics students.

2. The author of Text A is Alfred Marshall (1842—1924). Marshall's influence on modifying economic thought is difficult to deny. He popularized the use of supply and demand functions as tools of price determination. Modern economists owe the linkage between price

115

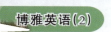

shifts and curve shifts to Marshall. Marshall was an important part of the "marginalist revolution." The idea that consumers attempt to adjust consumption until marginal utility equals the price was another of his contributions.

3. Measure Unit—Shilling: a cupronickel coin and former monetary unit of the United Kingdom, the 20th part of a pound, equal to 12 pence, shortened as "s."
lb stands for "pound," a unit of weight, an avoirdupois unit of weight equal to 7,000 grains, divided into 16 ounces (0.453 kg), used for ordinary commerce.

Task 1   Generating the Outline

Directions: Please identify the thesis of the passage and the main point of each paragraph and find out how these points develop the thesis. You may use the table below to help you.

The Thesis:	The ultimate regulator of all demands is _____.
Para. 1: **The phenomenon:**	A trader's or a manufacturer's demand is based on _____. The price a trader or a manufacturer can afford to buy a thing depends on _____.
Para. 2: **The basic concept:**	_____, which is correlative to Desire or Want, refers to the resulting satisfaction from the purchase.
Para. 3: **Analysis of wants:**	Wants, though in great variety, has a _____, which is called _____, or _____.
Paras. 4—6: **A new term and the law:**	_____ is something that a person is only just induced to purchase. The marginal utility of a thing to anyone _____. Implicit condition: no change in the _____ of the man himself.
Paras. 7—9: **Illustration and rewording of the law:**	The price which lies at the margin of one's purchase is called _____. The larger the amount of a thing a person has the lower, other things being equal, his _____.

Task 2   Understanding the Text

Direction: Please answer the following questions based on Text A.

1. From a long term of view, what determines a trader's willingness to pay for a thing? (Para. 1)
2. What does the author say about the nature of Desire or Want? (Para. 2)
3. How does the author characterize "Wants" in Paragraph 3?
4. Does an additional increase of one's stock always bring people satisfaction? (Para. 3)
5. What does the author mean by "marginal purchase"? (Para. 4)
6. What's the first law proposed by the author? How do you understand it?
7. What's the precondition for the first law proposed by the author? (Para. 6)

8. How does the author illustrate the law? Could you give another example? (Para. 7)
9. What does the author mean by "marginal demand price"? (Para. 8)
10. What's the precondition for the second law proposed by the author? (Para. 9)

Task 3 Vocabulary Building

Directions: Work in pairs or groups. Use a corpus to find out how frequently each of the following words appears in different text types. An example is given for you to follow. Then discuss the implications of the results.

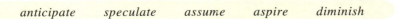

anticipate   speculate   assume   aspire   diminish

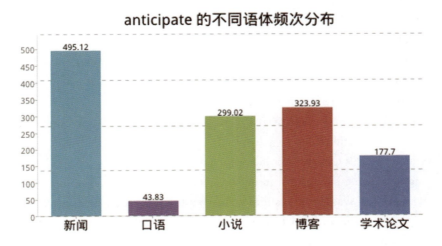

Text types	Frequency (每百万句频次)	Example
News	495.12	Did the U.S. anticipate this? Do you anticipate that happening? Don't anticipate any of this too soon.
Spoken	43.83	As I had anticipated, so it happened. In short, I had every reason to anticipate a perfect recovery.
Novels	299.02	I anticipate no conflict with them. I anticipate no such horrible event.
Blogs	323.93	It's about anticipating future. Investors are anticipating even more.
Academic papers	177.70	Similar morbidity can be anticipated between the two groups. These complications should be anticipated and treated in time. Various objections to this thesis are anticipated and answered.

(来源：句酷批改网语料库字典之"语体对比"部分，www.pigai.org)

Task 4 Learning the Phrases

Directions: Please fill in the blanks in the sentences below with the phrases listed in the box. Change the form if necessary. Notice that some phrases need to be used more than once.

derive from	in the long run	give rise to	in general
be concerned with	correspond to	at a rate	feed on

1. It is difficult to imagine a butterfly without a plant to _____, and we have to assume that both the plants and the appropriate pollinators diversified together.
2. In one way or another almost all the world's energy resources _____ the sun.
3. The possibility that some fossils _____ species no longer alive today had been noted even in the late seventeenth century.
4. The personal social services _____ a range of services for children and for elderly, mentally disordered and physically disabled people.
5. Once established, the plant will produce long stems, _____ numerous shoots.
6. Whether they can increase production _____ which allows urban markets to be fed and exports to be maintained depends on several factors.
7. On the demand side, we may treat the two goods as _____ investment and consumption goods (identical in production).
8. Sharks have huge oily livers, which increase buoyancy, but _____ they are obliged to keep swimming to provide enough lift to avoid sinking.
9. In Britain, while there was little institutional separation of sociology, there was a sociological tradition _____ the work of Herbert Spencer.
10. There is a definition of peace that _____ may be more rewarding than any other: Peace is opportunity.

Task 5 Studying the Sentence Structure

A. Predicative Clause

A sentence from the text:

It is that we do not suppose time to be allowed for any alteration in the character or tastes of the man himself.

Instructions: In the above sentence, "is" is a link verb. After the conjunction "that," there is a complete sentence. The sentence is called predicative clause. The basic sentence structure of this type of sentences is "subject + link verb +(that)+ predicative clause." The link verbs could be "be," "look," "remain," "seem" etc. The conjunction "that" could be omitted. More examples are provided below. Can you give more examples?

1. It seems **that it is going to rain**.
2. That is **why Jane got fired**.
3. Tomorrow is **when it would be most convenient**.
4. Home is **where the heart is**.
5. The reason he did not come is **that he was sick**.
6. The question **remains whether we can persuade her to join us**.

Unit 6

B. Appositive Clause

A sentence from the text:

While the fact that he does not buy an eleventh pound, shows that he does not think that it would be worth an extra 2s. to him.

Instructions: In the above sentence, the sentence "he does not buy an eleventh pound" after "the fact" and the conjunction "that" gives further explanation about the noun "fact." The sentence is an appositive. Besides "that," the conjunction could also be "what" "which" "who" "when" "where" "why" "how" "whether" or "if". Examples are:

1. The news **that we are invited to the conference** is very exciting.
2. There arose the question **where we could get the loan**.
3. A story goes **that the emperor was killed by his son**.
4. It is not a question **whether his is dependable**.
5. An idea came to him **that he might write the paper in another way**.

Below is a list of nouns that could be followed by an appositive. Can you use them to make some sentences with appositives?

belief	hope	idea	doubt	news	rumor	conclusion	evidence	order
decision	view	rule	advice	dream	proof	probability	demand	request
desire	concept	notion	ground	chance	assertion			

Task 6 Paraphrasing Difficult Sentences

1. When a trader or a manufacturer buys anything to be used in production, or be sold again, his demand is based on his anticipations of the profits which he can derive from it. (Para. 1)

   _____
   _____

2. It has been already argued that desires cannot be measured directly, but only indirectly by the outward phenomena to which they give rise: and that in those cases with which economics is chiefly concerned the measure is found in the price which a person is willing to pay for the fulfilment or satisfaction of his desire. (Para. 2)

   _____
   _____

3. He may have desires and aspirations which are not consciously set for any satisfaction: but for the present we are concerned chiefly with those which do so aim. (Para. 2)

   _____
   _____

4. That part of the thing which he is only just induced to purchase may be called his marginal purchase, because he is on the margin of doubt whether it is worth his while to incur the outlay required to obtain it.(Para. 4)

   _____
   _____

5. There is however an implicit condition in this law which should be made clear. It is that we do not suppose time to be allowed for any alteration in the character or tastes of the man himself.(Para. 6)

Task 7 Summarizing the Text

Direction: Please summarize Text A in about 100 words. You may use the table in Task 1 to help you.

Task 8 Writing with Rigorous Logic
Example from the text

The marginal utility of a thing to anyone diminishes with every increase in the amount of it he already has.

There is however an implicit condition in this law which should be made clear. It is that we do not suppose time to be allowed for any alteration in the character or tastes of the man himself.

[The following explanation is adapted from Purdue OWL: https://owl.english.purdue.edu/owl/resource/659/01/.]

Instructions: Logic is a formal system of analysis that helps writers invent, demonstrate, and prove arguments. It works by testing propositions against one another to determine their accuracy. People often think they are using logic when they avoid emotion or make arguments based on their common sense, such as "Everyone should look out for their own self-interests" or "People have the right to be free." However, unemotional or common sense statements are not always equivalent to logical statements. To be logical, a proposition must be tested within a logical sequence.

The most famous logical sequence, called the **syllogism**, was developed by the Greek philosopher Aristotle. His most famous syllogism is:

Premise 1: All men are mortal.

Premise 2: Socrates is a man.

Conclusion: Therefore, Socrates is mortal.

In this sequence, premise 2 is tested against premise 1 to reach the logical conclusion. Within this system, if both premises are considered valid, there is no other logical conclusion than determining that Socrates is a mortal.

Crafting a logical sequence into a written argument can be a very difficult task. Don't assume that an audience will easily follow the logic that seems clear to you. When converting logica

syllogisms into written arguments, remember to:
- lay out each premise clearly
- provide evidence for each premise
- draw a clear connection to the conclusion

In the above example from the text, the law is worded as "The marginal utility of a thing to anyone diminishes with every increase in the amount of it he already has." The conclusion does not stand watertight if the author does not continue to talk about the preconditions of the law.

Exercise: Finish the following conclusion and develop it into a 3-paragraph essay.

Premise 1: Minimum wage should match the cost of living in society.
Premise 2: The current minimum wage does not match the cost of living in society.
Conclusion: _____

Part Three   Reading and Speaking

Text B

Yes, the Wealthy Can Be Deserving
N. Gregory Mankiw

In 2012, the actor Robert Downey Jr., played the role of Tony Stark, **a.k.a.** Iron Man, in "The Avengers." For his work in that single film, Mr. Downey was paid an astounding(使人震惊的) $50 million.

Does that fact make you mad? Does his **compensation strike you as** a great injustice? Does it make you want to take to the streets in protest? These questions go to the heart of the debate over economic inequality, to which President Obama has recently been drawing attention.

Certainly, $50 million is a lot of money. The typical American would have to work for about 1,000 years in order to earn that much.

That sum puts Mr. Downey in the top ranks of American earners. Anything more than about $400,000 a year puts you in the much-talked-about 1 percent. If you earn more than about $10 million, you are in the top 1 percent of the top 1 percent. Mr. Downey makes it easily.

Yet, somehow, when I talk to people about it, most are not astounded by his income. Why?

One reason seems to be that they understand how he earned it. "The Avengers" was a blockbuster(大片) with worldwide box-office **receipts** of more than $1.5 billion. Of that amount, only about 3 percent went to pay Mr. Downey. In other words, if you bought a matinee(午场)movie ticket for, say, $8, about 25 cents went to pay for

Mr. Downey's acting. If you have seen the movie, you might be *tempted* to say: "He gave a great performance. I'm happy to pay him a quarter for it."

8   People are similarly unperturbed（泰然自若的）when they learn that in 2013, E. L. James, author of the "Fifty Shades of Grey" trilogy（三部曲）, earned $95 million, or that in the same year the basketball star LeBron James earned $56 million in salary and *endorsements*. When people can see with their own eyes that a talented person made a great fortune *fair and square*, they tend not to *resent* it.

9   But actors, authors, and athletes do not make up the entire ranks of the rich. Most top earners make their fortunes in ways that are less *transparent* to the public.

10   Consider chief executives. Without doubt, they are paid handsomely, and their pay has grown over time relative to that of the average worker. In 2012, the *median* pay of C.E.O.'s for companies in the Standard & Poor's 500-stock index was nearly $10 million. Did they deserve it?

11   *Critics* sometimes suggest that this high pay reflects the failure of *corporate* boards to do their job. Rather than representing shareholders, this argument goes, those boards are too *cozy* with the chief executives and pay them more than they are really worth.

12   Yet this argument fails to explain the behavior of closely held corporations. A private equity（股票）group with a controlling interest in a firm does not face this supposed *principal*-agent problem between shareholders and boards, and yet these closely held firms also pay their chief executives similarly high compensation. *In light of* this, the most natural explanation of high C.E.O. pay is that the value of a good C.E.O. is extraordinarily high.

13   That is hardly a surprise. A typical chief executive is *overseeing* billions of dollars of shareholder wealth as well as thousands of employees. The value of making the right decisions is *tremendous*. Just consider the role of Steve Jobs in the rise of Apple and its path-breaking products.

14   A similar case is the finance industry, where many large compensation *packages* can be found. There is no doubt that this *sector* plays a crucial economic role. Those who work in banking, *venture* capital（风险投资）and other financial firms are *in charge of allocating* the economy's investment resources. They decide, in a decentralized and competitive way, which companies and industries will *shrink* and which will grow. It makes sense that a nation would allocate many of its most talented and thus highly compensated individuals to the task.

15   In addition, recent research establishes that those working in finance face particularly risky incomes. Greater risk requires greater reward.

16   To be sure, some people find ways to get rich at others' expense. Bernard Madoff most famously comes to mind. The solution here, however, is not to focus on the income *distribution* but to *devise* better regulation and *oversight*.

17   A reliable tax system is also important to ensure that the wealthy pay their fair share to support the public *weal*. That is generally the case. Our tax system is far from

perfect and is *arguably* in *dire* need of reform, but examples of the tax *dodging* wealthy are not at all the *norm*.

The Tax Policy Center estimates that in 2013, the top one-tenth of 1 percent of the income distribution, those earning more than $2.7 million, paid 33.8 percent of their income in federal taxes. By contrast, the middle class, defined as the middle fifth of the income distribution, paid just 12.4 percent.

So, by delivering extraordinary performances in *hit* films, top stars may do more than entertain millions of moviegoers and make themselves rich in the process. They may also contribute many millions in federal taxes, and other millions in state taxes. And those millions help fund schools, police departments and national defense for the rest of us.

Unlike the superheroes of "The Avengers," the richest 1 percent aren't motivated by an altruistic(无私的)desire to advance the public good. But, in most cases, that is precisely their effect.

(901 words)

New Words

a.k.a		abbr.	also known as 又叫做, 亦称
compensation	[ˌkɒmpenˈseɪʃn]	n.	sth. given or received as an equivalent for services, debt, loss, injury, suffering, lack, etc. 报酬
receipt	[rɪˈsiːt]	n.	the amount or quantity received 收入
tempt	[tempt]	v.	to render strongly disposed to do sth. 倾向于
endorsement	[ɪnˈdɔːsmənt]	n.	the placing of one's signature, instructions, etc., on a document 代言
resent	[rɪˈzent]	v.	to feel or show displeasure or indignation at (a person, act, remark, etc.) from a sense of injury or insult 对……感到愤怒, 怨恨, 愤恨; 厌恶
transparent	[trænsˈpærənt]	a.	easily seen through, recognized, or detected 公开的
median	[ˈmiːdɪən]	n.	the middle number in a given sequence of numbers, taken as the average of the two middle numbers when the sequence has an even number of numbers 中位数
critic	[ˈkrɪtɪk]	n.	a person who judges, evaluates, or criticizes 评论家
corporate	[ˈkɔːpərət]	a.	of, for, or belonging to a corporation or corporations 企业的
cozy	[ˈkəʊzɪ]	a.	avoiding or not offering challenge or difficulty 不提出挑战的

principal	[ˈprɪnsəpl]	n.	a person who authorizes another, as an agent, to represent him or her 委托人
oversee	[ˌəʊvəˈsiː]	v.	to supervise; manage 监督，监视
tremendous	[trəˈmendəs]	a.	extraordinarily great in size, amount, or intensity 巨大的
package	[ˈpækɪdʒ]	n.	a group, combination, or series of related parts or elements to be accepted or rejected as a single unit 一揽子计划
sector	[ˈsektə]	n.	a distinct part, especially of society or of a nation's economy 部门，部分
venture	[ˈventʃə]	n.	a business enterprise or speculation in which sth is risked in the hope of profit 冒险，投机
allocate	[ˈæləkeɪt]	v.	to set apart for a particular purpose; assign or allot 分配
shrink	[ʃrɪŋk]	v.	to contract or lessen in size 缩小，萎缩
distribution	[ˌdɪstrɪˈbjuːʃn]	n.	an act or instance of distributing 分配
devise	[dɪˈvaɪz]	v.	to contrive, plan, or elaborate; invent from existing principles or ideas 设计，发明，策划，想出
oversight	[ˈəʊvəsaɪt]	n.	supervision; watchful care 监督
weal	[wiːl]	n.	well-being, prosperity, or happiness 幸福
arguably	[ˈɑːɡjʊəbli]	ad.	to being supported by convincing or persuasive argument 可论证地，可争辩地
dire	[ˈdaɪə]	a.	urgent; desperate 迫切的
dodge	[dɒdʒ]	v.	to elude or evade by a sudden shift of position or by strategy 闪躲，回避
norm	[nɔːm]	n.	a standard, model, or pattern 标准，规范，准则
hit	[hɪt]	n.	anything very successful and popular 成功之物

Phrases & Expressions

strike sb. as	to affect someone in a certain way 给人某种印象
fair and square	honest; just; straightforward 公平合理
in light of	according to; based on 根据
in charge of	having the care or supervision of 负责

 **Notes**

1. This passage was published in *The New York Times*, on February 16, 2014.
2. N. Gregory Mankiw (1958—) is Professor of Economics at Harvard University. As a student, he studied economics at Princeton University and MIT. As a teacher, he has taught macroeconomics, microeconomics, statistics, and principles of economics. Professor Mankiw is a prolific writer and a regular participant in academic and policy debates. He has written two popular textbooks—the intermediate-level textbook *Macroeconomics* (Worth Publishers) and the introductory textbook *Principles of Economics* (South-Western/Thomson). *Principles of Economics* has sold over a million copies and has been translated into twenty languages including Chinese. (Adapted from Professor Mankiw's official webpage: http://scholar.harvard.edu/mankiw/content/biography-60)
3. closely held corporation: a corporation in which more than half of the shares are held by five or fewer individuals. Closely held corporations are private companies, and are not publicly held. A closely held corporation is a private corporation, but a private corporation may or may not be closely held. In a closely held corporation, the management of the business may overlap with the primary shareholders.

Task 1 Oral Summarizing

Section 1 Listing People

Directions: List the people given by the author who earn a lot yet at the same time do not surprise average people. What do they do to get such a handsome pay? You may first fill in the blanks and then use your own words to speak out. Make it a coherent speech.

Name/Position	How much he earns/they earn	What he does/they do
Robert Downey Jr.		

Section 2 Listing Figures

Directions: The author recommends a reliable tax system to regulate the distribution of wealth. How does he explain that "Examples of the tax dodging wealthy are not at all the norm"?(Para. 17) Make a list of the figures the author gives and speak out in your own words.

Task 2 Synthesizing Information

Directions: Price is the amount of money you have to pay for something. It may go up or drop. In this unit, all of the two listening tasks and two reading tasks, in one way or another, deal with the factors that affect price. In the following table, first summarize the information relating to pricing from each task and then synthesize the factors that may affect price and speak out.

Tasks	Factors
Audio listening: Behind the Price Rise of Rice	
Video watching: Global Wealth Inequality	
Reading Text A: Gradations of Consumers' Demand	
Reading Text B: Yes, the Wealthy Can Be Deserving	

Task 3 Making Comments

Section 1 Thinking Critically

Directions: In Text B, as a republican, Mankiw argues that the wealthy could be deserving, amounting to a defense of inequality in American society. Do you think his arguments are water-tight? What possible counter arguments could you put forward? You may refer to Michael Tomasky's article "Greg Mankiw: the Wealthy are 'Deserving,' Even When They're Crooks" (Published on The Daily Beast on Feb. 17, 2014) for some ideas.

Mankiw's example	possible counter arguments
The value of a good CEO is extraordinarily high.	
No one he asks about Robert Downey Jr.'s making $50 million for "The Avengers" seems to resent his compensation.	

Section 2 Solving Problems

Directions: Some products can be highly-priced but others cannot. A few people have accumulated a large fortune but a lot are struggling for survival. Wealth inequality can be more harmful than expected. What leads to wealth inequality? What may be your suggested solutions to it? In groups articulate the problems and give as many detailed solutions as possible. You can either target problems presented in this unit or talk about problems from your own world knowledge. Then in class, present your comments.

problems	solutions

Part Four Cross Cultural Communication

Passage A

泛论生产事业

陈焕章 著 韩华 译

中国人很早就以劳动分工原则为基础,将人们划分为四类。这样的分类并非种姓制度,而是在职业上的区分,包括了所有人。《穀梁传》上说:"古者有四民,有士民,有商民,有农民,有工民。"

何休给四民的定义为:"古者有四民,一曰德能居位曰士;二曰辟土殖谷曰农;三曰巧心劳手以成器物曰工;四曰通财鬻货曰商。四民不相兼,然后财用足。"这是古人的分类体系,我们今天仍在使用。

在孔子思想的影响下,中国不存在社会阶级与种姓制度。但是,根据劳动分工,中国曾经有,现在也有四民。仅从以上所引材料的陈述中,我们注意到具有特殊意义的三点。第一,社会平等,士、农、工、商均一视同仁谓之为民,即四民平等;第二,商与士、农、工一样,他们均具有生产性。在汉语里,"四民"的排序通常为:士为四民之首,其次是农,再其次是工,最后是商。然而,根据《穀梁传》,商人却仅次于士人。显而易见,孔教徒认可商人所具有的生产性,无论商在四民中居第二,或居第四,他们并不因此对商人不友善。第三是劳动分工的原则。划分"四民"的目的是使生产力量更加充分,而且,民众并未被限制在任何被指定的职业类别之中,而只是通过职业分类被划分为某一类"民"。以上所述均是划分四民体系的实质。

关于四民在古代存在的静态的理论。据管子所论,"昔圣王之处士也,使就闲燕;处工,就官府;处商,就市井;处农,就田野……其事君者言敬,其幼者言弟。少而习焉,其心安焉,不见异物而迁焉。是故其父兄之教不肃而成;其子弟之学不劳而能"。这样,每类"民"之子孙通常继续从事其父辈的职业。因此,四民应该分开居住,"勿使杂处,杂处则其言哤,其事易"。管子成功地贯彻了"四民"分开居住的理论,而且,该理论与孔教徒的理论一致。事实上,分开"四民"的目的并非为了社会差别,而是为了职业专门化。

(739 字)

注解

1. 本篇节选自陈焕章著的 *The Economic Principles of Confucius and His School*(《孔门理财学》),由韩华翻译。2010年由中华书局出版。选文页码为233—234。
2. 陈焕章(1881—1933),字重远,广东高要人。早年入万木草堂受业于康有为。光绪三十三年(1904)中进士,1907年赴美国哥伦比亚大学经济系留学,1911年获经济学博士学位。1912年发起成立孔教会,自任主任干事。1923年任北京孔教大学校长。1930年在香港创立孔教学院,自任院长。

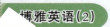

Word Bank

劳动分工	division of labor	职业专门化	professionalization
士民	scholar	孔子思想	Confucian thoughts

Directions: Please summarize the passage in English. Your summary should be about 150—200 words.

_____
_____
_____
_____
_____
_____
_____
_____

Passage B

Of the Origin and Use of Money

Adam Smith

When the division of labour has been once thoroughly established, it is but a very small part of a man's wants which the produce of his own labour can supply. He supplies the far greater part of them by exchanging that surplus part of the produce of his own labour, which is over and above his own consumption, for such parts of the produce of other men's labour as he has occasion for. Every man thus lives by exchanging, or becomes in some measure a merchant, and the society itself grows to be what is properly a commercial society. But when the division of labour first began to take place, this power of exchanging must frequently have been very much clogged and embarrassed in its operations. One man, we shall suppose, has more of a certain commodity than he himself has occasion for, while another has less. The former consequently would be glad to dispose of, and the latter to purchase, part of this superfluity. But if this latter should chance to have nothing that the former stands in need of, no exchange can be made between them. The butcher has more meat in his shop than he himself can consume, and the brewer and the baker would each of them be willing to purchase a part of it. But they have nothing to offer in exchange, except the different productions of their respective trades, and the butcher is already provided with all the bread and beer which he has immediate occasion for. No exchange can, in this case, be made between them. He cannot be their merchant, nor they his customers; and they are all of them thus mutually less serviceable to one another. In order to avoid the inconveniency of such situations, every prudent man in every period of society, after the first establishment of the division of labour, must naturally have endeavoured to manage his affairs in such a manner as to have at all times by him, besides the peculiar produce of his own industry, a certain quantity of some one commodity or other, such as he imagined few people would be likely to refuse in exchange for the produce of their industry.

Many different commodities, it is probable, were successively both thought of and employed for this purpose. In the rude ages of society, cattle are said to have been the common instrument of commerce; and, though they must have been a most inconvenient one, yet in old times we find things were frequently valued according to the number of cattle which had been given in exchange for them. The armour of Diomede, says Homer, cost only nine oxen; but that of Glaucus cost an hundred oxen. Salt is said to be the common instrument of commerce and exchanges in Abyssinia; a species of shells in some parts of the coast of India; dried cod at Newfoundland; tobacco in Virginia; sugar in some of our West India colonies; hides or dressed leather in some other countries; and there is at this day a village in Scotland where it is not uncommon, I am told, for a workman to carry nails instead of money to the baker's shop or the alehouse.

In all countries, however, men seem at last to have been determined by irresistible reasons to give the preference, for this employment, to metals above every other commodity. Metals can not only be kept with as little loss as any other commodity, scarce anything being less perishable than they are, but they canlikewise, without any loss, be divided into any number of parts, as by fusion those parts can easily be reunited again; a quality which no other equally durable commodities possess, and which more than any other quality renders them fit to be the instruments of commerce and circulation.

The man who wanted to buy salt, for example, and had nothing but cattle to give in exchange for it, must have been obliged to buy salt to the value of a whole ox, or a whole sheep at a time. He could seldom buy less than this, because what he was to give for it could seldom be divided without loss; and if he had a mind to buy more, he must, for the same reasons, have been obliged to buy double or triple the quantity, the value, to wit, of two or three oxen, or of two or three sheep. If, on the contrary, instead of sheep or oxen, he had metals to give in exchange for it, he could easily proportion the quantity of the metal to the precise quantity of the commodity which he had immediate occasion for.

(779 words)

 **Notes**

1. This passage was excerpted from *The Wealth of Nations Book I*.
2. Adam Smith (1723—1790) was a Scottish moral philosopher, pioneer of political economy, and key Scottish Enlightenment figure. He is best known for two classic works: *The Theory of Moral Sentiments* (1759), and *An Inquiry into the Nature and Causes of the Wealth of Nations* (1776). The latter, usually abbreviated as *The Wealth of Nations*, is considered his master piece and the first modern work of economics. Smith is cited as the "father of modern economics" and is still among the most influential thinkers in the field of economics today.

Directions: Please summarize the passage in Chinese. Your summary should be about 200—300 words.

Unit 7

BETWEEN TWO WORLDS

From space, we see a small and fragile ball—dominated not by human activity and edifice but a pattern of clouds, oceans, greenery, and soils. Humanity's inability to fit its activities into that pattern is changing planetary systems, fundamentally. Many such changes are accompanied by life-threatening hazards. This new reality, from which there is no escape, must be recognized and managed.

—From "From One Earth to One World" of Our Common Future, the Report of the World Commission on Environment and Development of United Nations

Learning Objectives

Upon completion of this unit, you should be able to:

Remember & Understand	★ recognize and retrieve terms related to environmental protection; ★ identify and explain in your own words the thesis and the major points of Text A and Text B;
Analyze & Apply	★ use corpora to learn the collocational patterns of a new word; ★ make reference to the thesis and the major points of Text A and Text B in your writing; ★ produce sentences with ellipsis; ★ use fronting and inversion for emphasis;
Evaluate & Create	★ use sensory words in descriptive paragraphs; ★ synthesize information about the environmental protection from related sources; ★ deliver a clear and coherent oral presentation of your views on the relationship between environmental protection and economic development.

Part One Lead-in

Section 1 Listening

Task 1 Filling the Blanks

Directions: Please fill in the blanks with one or two words on the basis of what you have heard in "Human Price."

Where do pesticides fit into the picture of ___1___ disease? We have seen that they now contaminate soil, water, and food, that they have the power to make our streams fishless and our gardens and woodlands silent and birdless. Man, however much he may like to pretend the contrary, is part of nature. Can he escape a pollution that is now so ___2___ distributed throughout our world?

We know that even single ___3___ to these chemicals, if the amount is large enough, can precipitate acute poisoning.

But this is not the major problem. The sudden illness or death of farmers, spraymen, pilots, and others exposed to ___4___ quantities of pesticides are tragic and should not occur. For the population as a whole, we must be more ___5___ the delayed effects of absorbing small amounts of the pesticides that invisibly contaminate our world.

Responsible public health officials have pointed out that the ___6___ effects of chemicals are cumulative over long periods of time, and that the hazard to the individual may ___7___ the sum of the exposures received throughout his lifetime. For these very reasons the danger is easily ___8___. It is human nature to ___9___ what may seem to us a vague threat of future disaster. "Men are naturally most impressed by diseases which have ___10___ manifestations," says a wise physician, Dr. René Dubos, "yet some of their worst enemies creep on them unobtrusively."

Task 2 Group Discussion

Please discuss the following questions in pairs or groups based on what you have heard.

1. According to the audio, what's the real danger of chemicals such as pesticides for human beings?
2. Can you describe the positive and negative effects of one chemical you use everyday?
3. What is your attitude towards chemicals?

Section 2 Watching

Task 1 Group Discussion

Directions: Please watch the video "Wheatgrass in Shapotou" and discuss the following questions in pairs or groups.

1. How is Shapotou's environment according to the video?
2. What's the Soviet Union's protection measure for the railway? And how is its effect?
3. What's the effective solution to protect the land in Shapotou?

Task 2 Imitation

Directions: Please watch the video again, and introduce your hometown following the example below.

Shapotou lies at 16 kilometers to the northwest of Zhongwei. The Yellow River makes a huge "S" turn here, cutting through 100-meter-high sand hill right in the middle. Shapotou means head of the sandy slope.

Part Two Reading and Writing

Text A

The World We Have Lost
James Gustave Speth

Half the world's tropical and temperate forests are now gone. The rate of deforestation in the *tropics* continues at about an acre a second. About half the wetlands and a third of the mangroves(红树) are gone. An estimated 90 percent of the large *predator* fish are gone, and 75 percent of *marine* fisheries are now overfished or fished to *capacity*. Twenty percent of the corals are gone, and another 20 percent severely threatened. *Species* are disappearing at rates about a thousand times faster than normal. The planet has not seen such a spasm of(一阵)extinction in sixty-five million years, since the dinosaurs disappeared. Over half the agricultural land in drier regions suffers from some degree of deterioration(恶化) and desertification. Persistent toxic chemicals can now be found by the dozens in essentially each and every one of us.

Human impacts are now large relative to natural systems. The earth's stratospheric ozone layer(平流臭氧层) was severely *depleted* before the change was discovered. Human activities have pushed *atmospheric* carbon dioxide up by more than a third and have started in earnest the dangerous process of warming the planet and disrupting climate. Everywhere earth's ice fields are melting. Industrial processes are fixing nitrogen(氮气), making it biologically active, at a rate equal to nature's; one result is the development of more than two hundred dead zones in the oceans *due to* overfertilization. Human actions already *consume* or destroy each year about 40 percent of nature's photosynthetic(光合作用的)output, leaving too little for other species. Freshwater *withdrawals* doubled globally between 1960 and 2000, and are now over half of *accessible* runoff(径流量). The following rivers no longer reach the oceans in the dry season: the Colorado, Yellow, Ganges, and Nile, among others.

Societies are now traveling together in the midst of this *unfolding calamity* down a path that links two worlds. Behind is the world we have lost, ahead the world we are making.

4   It is difficult to appreciate the *abundance* of wild nature in the world we have lost. In America we can think of the pre-Columbian world of 1491, of Lewis and Clark, and of John James Audubon. It is a world where nature is large and we are not. It is a world of *majestic* old-growth forests stretching from the Atlantic to the Mississippi, of oceans *brimming* with fish, of clear skies literally darkened by passing *flocks* of birds. As William MacLeish notes in *The Day before America*, in 1602 an Englishman wrote in his journal that the fish schooled so thickly he thought their backs were the sea bottom. Bison once *roamed* east to Florida. There were jaguars in the Southeast, grizzly bear in the Midwest, and wolves, elk and mountain lions in New England.

5   Audubon described the breathtaking *multitudes* of the passenger pigeon *migration*, as well as the greed of their wild and human predators: "Few pigeons were to be seen before sunset; but a great number of persons, with horses and wagons, guns and ammunition, had already established camping grounels... Suddenly, there *burst forth* a general cry of 'Here they come!' The noise which they made, though yet distant, *reminded* me *of* a hard *gale* at sea...As the birds arrived, and passed over me, I felt a current of air that surprised me. Thousands were soon knocked down by polemen. The current of birds, however, still kept increasing...The pigeons, coming in by thousands, descended everywhere, one above another, until solid masses...were formed on every tree, in all directions. ... The *uproar* continues...the whole night. ... Toward the approach of day, the noise rather *subsided*. ... The howlings of the wolves now reached our ears; and the foxes, lynxes, cougars, bears, raccoons, opossums, and polecats were seen sneaking off from the spot. Whilst eagles and hawks, of different species, *accompanied* by a crowd of vultures, came to replace them, and enjoy their share of the *spoil*. It was then that the authors of all this devastation began their entry amongst the dead, the dying, and the torn. The pigeons were picked up and piled in heaps, until each had as many as he could possibly *dispose of*, when the hogs were let loose to feed on the *remainder*."

6   The last passenger pigeon on earth *expired* in a zoo in Cincinnati in 1914. Some decades later, forester and philosopher Aldo Leopold offered these words at a ceremony on this passing: "We grieve because no living man will see again the *onrushing* team of victorious birds, sweeping a path for spring across the March skies chasing the defeated winter from all the woods and *prairies*. ... Men still live who, in their youth, remember pigeons. Trees still live who, in their youth, were shaken by a living wind. ...There will always be pigeons in books and in museums, but these are effigies (雕像) and images, dead to all hardships and to all delights. Book-pigeon cannot dive out of a cloud to make the deer run for cover, or clap their wings in thunderous applause of mast-laden woods. Book-pigeons cannot breakfast on new-mown wheat in Minnesota and dine on blueberries in Canada. They know no urge of seasons; they feel no kiss of sun, no *lash* of wind and weather."

7   Human societies are moving, rapidly now, between the two worlds. The movement began slowly, but now we are rushing toward the world directly ahead. The old world

nature's world, continues, of course, but we are steadily closing it down, *roping* it *off*. It *flourishes* in our art and literature and in our imaginations. But it is disappearing.

(956 words)

New Words

tropics	[ˈtrɒpɪks]	n.	the hottest area of the Earth, between the Tropic of Cancer and the Tropic of Capricorn 热带地区
predator	[ˈpredətə]	n.	an animal that hunts, kills and eats other animals 捕食性动物，食肉动物
marine	[məˈriːn]	a.	related to the sea or sea transport 海(洋)的；航海的；海运的
capacity	[kəˈpæsəti]	n.	the total amount that can be contained or produced, or (esp. of a person or organization) the ability to do a particular thing 容积，容量；生产能力；(尤指某人或某组织的)办事能力
species	[ˈspiːʃiːz]	n.	a set of animals or plants in which the members have similar characteristics to each other and can breed with each other(动植物的)种，物种
deplete	[dɪˈpliːt]	v.	to reduce sth. in size or amount, esp. supplies of energy, money, etc. 消耗，耗费，减少
atmospheric	[ˌætməsˈferɪk]	a.	relating to the air or to the atmosphere 空气的；大气(层)的
consume	[kənˈsjuːm]	v.	to use fuel, energy or time, esp. in large amounts (尤指大量地)消耗，消费，花费
withdrawal	[wɪðˈdrɔːəl]	n.	when a military force moves out of an area 撤军
accessible	[əkˈsesəbl]	a.	able to be reached or easily got 可进入的，可接近的，可得到的
unfold	[ʌnˈfəʊld]	v.	to open or spread out sth. that has been folded 打开，展开，摊开
calamity	[kəˈlæmɪti]	n.	a serious accident or bad event causing damage or suffering 灾难，灾祸
abundance	[əˈbʌndəns]	n.	when there is more than enough of sth. 大量，充足，丰富
majestic	[məˈdʒestɪk]	a.	beautiful, powerful or causing great admiration and respect 雄伟的，壮丽的，威严的
brim	[brɪm]	v.	to become full of sth., esp. a liquid 注满，装满(尤指液体)

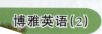

flock	[flɒk]	n.	a group of sheep, goats or birds, or a group of people 羊群；鸟群；人群
roam	[rəʊm]	v.	to move about or travel, esp. without a clear idea of what you are going to do 闲逛(于)，漫步(于)，漫游(于)
multitude	[ˈmʌltɪtjuːd]	n.	a large number of people or things 许多，众多
migration	[maɪˈgreɪʃən]	n.	when an animal migrates, it travels to a different place, usually when the season changes (动物)迁徙，移栖
gale	[geɪl]	n.	a very strong wind 大风
uproar	[ˈʌprɔːr]	n.	when a lot of people complain about sth. angrily 喧嚣，嘈杂，吵闹
subside	[səbˈsaɪd]	v.	to become less strong 较弱
accompany	[əˈkʌmpəni]	v.	to go with someone or to be provided or exist at the same time as sth. 陪同，陪伴；伴随，和……一起提供(或存在)
spoil	[spɔɪl]	n.	goods, advantages, profits, etc. that you get by your actions or because of your position or situation 战利品，掠夺物；权力、地位的连带利益，获益
remainder	[rɪˈmeɪndər]	n.	the part of sth. that is left after the other parts have gone, been used, or been taken away 剩余部分，其余，剩余物
expire	[ɪkˈspaɪər]	v.	if sth. which lasts for a fixed length of time expires, it comes to an end or stops being in use 到期，期满，结束
prairie	[ˈpreəri]	n.	a wide area of flat land without trees in Canada and the northern US (加拿大和美国北部的)大草原
lash	[læʃ]	v.	to hit with a lot of force 猛击，狠打
flourish	[ˈflʌrɪʃ]	v.	to grow or develop successfully 茁壮成长；繁荣，蓬勃发展

Phrases & Expressions

due to	because of 由于
burst forth	to break open or apart suddenly, or to make sth. do this 突发，爆发，迸发
remind of	to be similar to, and make you think of, sth. or someone else 类似于；使想起(类似的人或物)
dispose of	to get rid of someone or sth. or deal with sth. so that the matter is finished 清除；处理，解决；击败
rope off	to surround an area or place with ropes in order to keep people out 用绳围起，用绳索圈起

Unit 7

 **Notes**

1. The text was adapted from "Between Two Worlds," the introduction part of the book *The Bridge at the Edge of the World*. In this book, showing the environment has continued to decline to the point that humans are now at the edge of catastrophe, Gustave Speth contends that this situation is a severe indictment of the economic and political system humans call modern capitalism and points out the way to change the operating instructions for today's destructive world economy before it is too late.
2. The author of the book, James Gustave Speth (born on March 4, 1942) is a United States environmental lawyer and advocate, who is a founder of the Natural Resources Defense Council and World Resources Institute. Among his awards are the National Wildlife Federation's Resources Defense Award, the Natural Resources Council of America's Barbara Swain Award of Honor, the Lifetime Achievement Award of the Environmental Law Institute, and the Blue Planet Prize.

Task 1   Generating the Outline

Directions: Please identify the thesis of the passage and the main point of each paragraph and find out how these points develop the thesis. You may use the table below to help you.

The thesis:	The old world, nature's world, continues, of course, but we human beings are _____.
Para. 1: **The phenomenon:**	Natural environment is suffering _____.
Para. 2: **The reason:**	_____ are now large relative to natural systems' destruction.
Para. 3: **The position:**	Societies are now traveling together in the midst of this unfolding calamity down a path that _____.
Para. 4: **The example:**	In the world we have lost, there was _____ wild nature resources.
Para. 5: **The description:**	Audubon described the breathtaking multitudes of _____, as well as the rapacity of their wild and human predators.
Para. 6: **The quotation:**	The last passenger pigeon on earth _____, resulting in pigeons' only living in books and in museums.
Para. 7: **The conclusion:**	The old world _____ in our art and literature and in our imaginations. But it is _____.

Task 2   Understanding the Text

Directions: Please answer the following questions based on Text A.

1. What are the "two worlds" in the passage?
2. Where are we humans standing now?

137

3. What's the author's attitude towards the lost world?
4. How is the current world we're living in? (Para. 1)
5. What are humanity's negative effects on the nature system? (Para. 2)
6. Why does the author mention William MacLeish's work in the passage? (Para. 4)
7. How does the author show the "breathtaking multitudes of the passenger pigeon migration"? (Para. 5)
8. What's the grief of human beings according to Aldo Leopold? (Para. 6)

Task 3 Vocabulary Building

Directions: Work in pairs or groups. Students in each pair or group should use different corpora or different parts of a same corpus to get the general collocational patterns of the words listed in the box. You should also obtain some most frequent specific collocational patterns of the words, as well as concordances illustrating each specific pattern. Compare the results with each other. An example is given below.

| accompany | consume | flourish | expire |
| majestic | withdrawal | spoil | unfold |

Accompany

Pattern		Concordances
general	specific	
accompany + n.	accompany team (8.69)	Ankiel did not accompany the team.
	accompany president (6.06)	Rubin accompanied the president.
	accompany story (3.88)	Photos will accompany both stories.
	accompany front (3.82)	A few light showers may accompany the front.
	accompany group (3.42)	Mrs. Mandela did not accompany the group.
n. + accompany	shower accompany (5.13)	A few light showers may accompany the front.
accompany + prep.	accompany to (26.73)	He accompanied them to the door.
	accompany on (23.04)	Jean accompanied her on the piano.
	accompany by (19.75)	Accompanied by MTV-VJS.
	accompany in (5.40)	His wife Paula will accompany him in a van.
	accompany at (2.30)	She was accompanied at the hearing by two dozen support.

accompany + v.-ing	accompany aging (0.46)	Weight lifting staves off the natural muscle-shriveling that accompanies.
	accompany Keating (0.26)	The Rev. Robert Rippy, who accompanied Keating to Rome, said the bishop died of a massive heart attack during the night.

(Source: www.pigai.org)

Task 4 Learning the Phrases

Directions: Please fill in the blanks in the sentences below with the phrases listed in the box. Change the forms if necessary. Notice that some phrases need to be used more than once.

> due to   flocks of   burst forth
> dispose of   feed on   rope off   remind of

1. How did they _____ the bodies after they won the war?
2. The Thames was in spate, with _____ Canada geese speeding downriver.
3. We _____ our dogs _____ fresh meat supplied by that factory.
4. It was a real prize _____ its rarity and good condition.
5. The eye _____ beautiful scenery: the sun arose and the fog rapidly dispersed, leaving a slight steam only to curl along the surface of the water.
6. It took a mere five minutes for the world champion to _____ his opponent.
7. _____ wet leaves on the line, this train will arrive an hour late.
8. Greed and shortsightedness didn't suddenly _____; they are constants of human nature.
9. The police _____ the scene of the crime.
10. Daytime television tended to _____ her too forcefully _____ her own situation.

Task 5 Studying the Sentence Structure

A. Fronting and Inversion

Sentences from the text

1. Behind is the world we have lost, ahead the world we are making. (Para. 3)

Directions: Please front some parts of the sentences below. Inverse the sentence when necessary.

Tips

> 1. Putting the element which should be in the latter part of the sentence in the front is called fronting, a way to highlight some parts.
> 2. Some fronting can cause inversion.
> 3. Subject complements in usual occasions are behind the subject, but when they are in the front of the sentence, they would cause inversion because of the long and complex subjects. Besides, when certain adverbials are fronted, inversion happens.

1. Those who receive great news of triumph after long silence are indeed happy.

2. A perfect answer will be found in this chapter.

3. I have never found him in such a gloomy mood.

B. Ellipsis

Sentences from the text

1. It is a world of majestic old-growth forests stretching from the Atlantic to the Mississippi, of oceans brimming with fish, of clear skies literally darkened by passing flocks of birds. (Para. 4)

2. Behind is the world we have lost, ahead the world we are making. (Para. 3)

Directions: Please delete some parts of the following sentences without changing the original meaning.

Tips

> 1. Ellipsis is a way to avoid redundancy and enhance coherence.
> 2. Some common elements or structures in the sentence can be omitted.

1. He has workers from China and workers from America in his company.

2. This is his first date with a beautiful girl and I hope it is not his last date with a beautiful girl.

3. Some books are to be tasted, others are to be swallowed, and some few are to be chewed and digested.

Task 6 Paraphrasing Difficult Sentences

1. The planet has not seen such a spasm of extinction in sixty-five million years, since the dinosaurs disappeared.

2. Societies are now traveling together in the midst of this unfolding calamity down a path that links two worlds.

3. It is a world of majestic old-growth forests stretching from the Atlantic to the Mississippi, of oceans brimming with fish, of clear skies literally darkened by passing flocks of birds.

4. The pigeons were picked up and piled in heaps, until each had as many as he could possibly dispose of, when the hogs were let loose to feed on the remainder.

5. There will always be pigeons in books and in museums, but these are effigies and images, dead to all hard ships and to all delights.

Task 7 Summarizing the Text

Directions: Please summarize Text A in 100 words. You may use the table in Task 1 to help you.

Task 8 Writing with Sensory Words

Directions: Write a passage of three paragraphs to show the change of natural environment in your life. You're supposed to describe the past and the present natural environments in the first two paragraphs and offer your comments on the change in the third paragraph. When writing about the natural environments, you need to use sensory words to describe what you see, hear, feel, touch and taste to form a contrast. You may use what is provided in the box below to help you. Your writing should be about 200 words.

Tips

1. Sensory words often stimulate the reader's imagination to form a sensory response from all five senses. In other words, a good description is expected to invite readers to see, hear, smell, taste and feel the things being described.

2. In Text A James Gustave Speth cited John James Audubon's description of "the breathtaking multitudes of the passenger pigeon migration, as well as the rapacity of their wild and human predators," in which Audubon used visual details such as "The pigeons, coming in by thousands, descended everywhere, one above another, until solid masses...were formed on every tree, in all directions," sound description such as "Suddenly, there burst forth a general cry of 'Here they come!' The noise which they made, though yet distant, reminded me of a hard gale at sea" and touch sense description such as "As the birds arrived, and passed over me, I felt a current of air that surprised me."

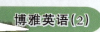

The village/ city/ community I lived in when I was a little kid was [...]
However, the environment has totally changed since [...]
In my opinion, [...]

Part Three Reading and Speaking

Text B

Saving the Amazon: Winning the war on deforestation
Justin Rowlatt

1   For years, the story told about the Amazon has been one of destruction—the world's largest rainforest, a region of amazing biodiversity, key to the fight against climate change, being mercilessly felled. But that is no longer the whole truth.

2   The Environment Agency special ops team gathered in a sultry(闷热的) town right on the southern edge of the Amazon. In Brazil, environment agents wear military *fatigues*, with heavy black pistols *slung* casually on their thighs.

3   I'd been invited along on one of the agency's *routine* raids in the jungle. The idea was to target a gang of illegal *loggers* the satellite monitoring team had *spotted* working in the forest.

4   On a map pinned to the wall, three commanders were working out strategies and *logistics*, just like a military operation. I was starting to feel *distinctly* anxious. "Are the loggers likely to be armed?" I asked. "Don't worry about guns," said the lead officer, Evandro Selva. "They're only likely to have hunting rifles. Nothing serious." Nothing serious?

5   Moments later, we were in a pickup truck on our way to the airstrip(简易机场) and before I knew it, Evandro was urging me into the helicopter, its blades already scything(高速穿过) through the humid air. I just had time to strap myself in before he gestured for *take-off* and the ground *shrank* away.

6   I was in Brazil to report on that rare thing, an environmental battle that is actually being won. For decades, pretty much the only story we've heard from the Amazon is about the remorseless tide of destruction sweeping through the forest. The received wisdom has always been that it is unstoppable. But I was here to discover the remarkable progress Brazil has made in silencing the chainsaws.

7   My journey was to take me across the southern Amazon, the area the Brazilians call "the arc of destruction"—a grey area between civilisation and one of the world's last true wildernesses. For years it was a *vision* of hell here. Vast fires swept through the forest while the chainsaws whined, and *armoured* tractors roared as they grubbed

up the roots of the great Amazonian trees.

An hour into our flight, Evandro signaled that we were nearing the target. We were over what looked to me like virgin jungle. There were still some trees standing—tall fragile-looking Brazil nut trees—but on the ground were great rough mounds of branches and brush. I could see open scars in the red earth where the machines had digged their passage. One of the officers pointed down. I saw a truck piled high with tree trunks and a tractor in front of it. We *wheeled* around and pilot started to bring the helicopter down. It kicked up a storm of dust and dry leaves. The rotors seemed dangerously close to the trees. I *hung on* tight.

Then we were on the ground and running. The truck and tractor were still there but, of course, the culprits had fled. "They'll be back," Evandro said confidently. "We'll just hide here and wait for them." The three officers hid among the logs and branches, pistols in their hands. I also took cover. Meanwhile, the helicopter flew off in another flurr of（一阵）of leaves and red earth. Then all was silent. Just we were *crouching* silently in the hot sun, clouds of tiny bees *swarming* around our faces and hands.

How can this possibly stop the deforestation, I thought to myself. In the decade between 1996 and 2005, 19,500 sq km (7,530 sq miles) of jungle was lost *on average* every single year. It reached a peak in 2004 when more than 27,000 sq km was lost. Then, in 2004 Brazil declared war—it said it would cut deforestation by 80% by 2020. Today it has almost reached its goal. The year of 2011 had the lowest rates of deforestation since records began three decades ago—just over 6,200 sq km was cut, still a lot of trees, but a huge improvement.

Of course, the Brazilian government cannot claim all the *credit*. On my journey I met a *bizarre* cast of characters all of whom are playing a role: John Carter, a Texan cayman(短吻鳄)-*wrestling* ex-US Special Forces soldier turned Amazonian rancher（大农场主）whose *alliance* of farmers and ranchers is working to improve land management on farms in the Amazon; the *indigenous* Amazonian Indians who have been recruited as "smoke jumpers"—forest fire-fighters; one of the most *efficient* agricultural enterprises on the planet—an Amazonian soya farm, who now claims to be an environmentalist; Greenpeace's adventurous pilot, a *veteran* of many of Greenpeace's successful *campaigns*.

But for the moment I was still hunched in the bushes, the first twinges of *cramp* in my leg and a river of sweat running down my back. We had been waiting half an hour when—just like in the movies—I heard a branch *snap* underfoot and suddenly the officers were up and running.

"Para ai! Para ai!" they shouted—"Stop right there!" I saw a man in a ragged T-shirt *dive into* the dirt, arms wide as if he had been crucified(钉在十字架上). Another hesitated on the edge of the forest. The officer in front of me fired his gun. The man turned and *darted off* into the trees.

In all, the officers arrested five men and impounded three trucks and two tractors. I'd been nervous about *confronting* these guys but they seemed rather *pathetic*, smoking rollups in their scruffy（邋遢的）clothes.

15　As we **bounced** back through the jungle, I couldn't help feeling a great sense of hope. Extraordinary as it sounds, it really does seem as if the war to stop the destruction of Amazon rainforest is being won. What's more this is happening before it is too late, because what most people don't realise is just how much of the forest is still standing. Satellite images **confirm** almost 80% of the Amazon is still **intact**.

(988 words)

New Words

fatigue	[fəˈtiːg]	n.	extreme tiredness 疲惫,劳累
sling	[slɪŋ]	v.	to throw or drop sth. carelessly(随便)扔,丢
routine	[ruːˈtiːn]	n.	a usual or fixed way of doing things 惯例,常规;例行公事
logger	[ˈlɒgə]	n.	a person who cuts down trees for wood 伐木工人,伐木者
spot	[spɒt]	v.	to mark with spots 弄上污渍
logistics	[ləˈdʒɪstɪks]	n.	the careful organization of a complicated activity so that it happens in a successful and effective way 后勤,后勤学
distinctly	[dɪˈstɪŋktli]	ad.	clearly noticeable; that certainly exists 显著地,明显地;确实地
take-off	[ˈteɪkˌɒf]	n.	when an aircraft leaves the ground and begins to fly 起飞,飞起
shrink	[ʃrɪŋk]	v.	to become smaller, or to make sth. smaller (使)缩小,(使)变小
vision	[ˈvɪʒən]	n.	an idea or mental image of sth. 头脑中的影像
armoured	[ˈɑːməd]	a.	protected by a strong covering, or using military vehicles protected by strong covering 装甲的;使用装甲车辆的,装配有装甲车辆的
wheel	[wiːl]	v.	to push an object that has wheels so that it moves in a particular direction 车轮滚动
crouch	[kraʊtʃ]	v.	to bend your knees and lower yourself so that you are close to the ground and leaning forward slightly 蹲下,蹲伏;蜷缩
swarm	[swɔːm]	n.	a large group of insects all moving together (一起移动的)一大群(昆虫)
credit	[ˈkredɪt]	n.	praise, approval or honour 赞扬,赞许;荣誉
bizzarre	[bɪˈzɑːr]	a.	very strange and unusual 怪诞的,罕见的;异乎寻常的

Unit 7

wrestle	[ˈresl]	v.	to fight with someone (esp. as a sport) by holding them and trying to throw them to the ground（尤指作为运动）（与……）摔跤，角力；（将……）摔倒
alliance	[əˈlaɪəns]	n.	a group of countries, political parties or people who have agreed to work together because of shared interests or aims 结盟国家（或团体），同盟国家（或团体）
indigenous	[ɪnˈdɪdʒɪnəs]	a.	naturally existing in a place or country rather than arriving from another place 当地的；本土的，土生土长的
efficient	[ɪˈfɪʃənt]	a.	working or operating quickly and effectively in an organized way 效率高的；有能力的；有效的；生效的
veteran	[ˈvetərən]	n.	someone who has been in the armed forces during a war 老兵，退伍军人
campaign	[kæmˈpeɪn]	n.	a planned group of esp. political, business or military activities which are intended to achieve a particular aim（尤指政治、商业或军事的）专项活动，运动
cramp	[kræmp]	v.	a sudden painful tightening in a muscle, often after a lot of exercise, which limits movement 痉挛，抽筋（常出现在大量运动后）
snap	[snæp]	v.	to cause sth. which is thin to break suddenly and quickly with a cracking sound 突然折断，咔嚓一声折断
confront	[kənˈfrʌnt]	v.	to face, meet or deal with a difficult situation or person 面对，面临；遭遇；直面，正视
pathetic	[pəˈθetɪk]	a.	causing feelings of sadness, sympathy or sometimes lack of respect, esp. because a person or an animal is suffering 招人怜悯的，可怜的
bounce	[baʊns]	v.	to (cause to) move up or away after hitting a surface（使）弹起，（使）反弹；反射；跳跃
confirm	[kənˈfɜːm]	v.	to make an arrangement or meeting certain, often by telephone or writing 确认，确定（安排或会议）
intact	[ɪnˈtækt]	a.	complete and in the original state 完整无缺的；未经触动的

145

take-off	when an aircraft leaves the ground and begins to fly 起飞，飞起
hang on	to hold 紧握
on average	the result you get by adding two or more amounts together and dividing the total by the number of amounts 平均数；平均
dive into	to start doing sth. suddenly and energetically, often without stopping to think 贸然投入到……之中
dart off	to move quickly or suddenly; escape quickly 飞快逃跑

1. This passage is adapted from "Saving the Amazom: Winning the war on deforestation," a report of Justin Rowlatt who is one of the main presenters of "Business Daily" on the BBC World Service.

2. Covering most of the Amazon Basin of South America, the Amazon, over half of the planet's remaining rainforests, comprises the largest and most biodiverse tract of tropical rainforest in the world, with an estimated 390 billion individual trees divided into 16,000 species, but it suffers from deforestation, the main sources of which are human settlement and development of the land, such as farming practices and the construction of transportation projects. The Amazon rainforest has being the one of the hottest environmental problems arousing the whole world's concerns.

Task 1　Summarizing

Directions: In this passage the reporter's attitudes towards environmental battle of Amazon change in the Environment Agency's jungle raid. Please fill in the blanks to summarize his different attitudes at different stages.

Different Stages	Attitudes
Before the jungle raid	
After the jungle raid	

Task 2　Synthesizing Information

Directions: In the modern time, the balance between nature and human is broken. Human's negative influences on nature are increasingly obvious as well as widespread. In this unit, the audio clip in Part One, Text A, and Text B, in one way or another exhibit human's destruction on nature. In the following table, first summarize the information relating to human's destruction from each part and then synthesize the negative effects that human exerts on nature. Speak the result out.

Tasks	Negative Effects
Audio listening: Human Price	
Reading Text A: The World We Have Lost	
Reading Text B: Saving the Amazon: Winning the war on deforestation	

Task 3 Making Comments

Directions: Please use the Amazon deforestation as a case study to explore the causes for we human's ruining the natural balance and give as many detailed solutions as possible. You can have a discussion with your group members, and then present your comments.

Tips

1. Reliable sources may include examples, research results, statistics, etc.
2. Amazon deforestation involves different roles such as the operation team, the illegal loggers, local ranchers, enterprises, international organisations and the reporter who represent different standpoints and interest groups. So you need to investigate the causes rooted in these interest groups to form a comprehensive understanding of the Amazon problem and then accordingly find the appropriate solutions.

Causes	Solutions

Comments

_____
_____
_____
_____
_____
_____

Part Four Cross Cultural Communication

Passage A

大气污染防治行动计划

　　大气环境保护事关人民群众根本利益,事关经济持续健康发展,事关全面建成小康社会,事关实现中华民族伟大复兴中国梦。当前,我国大气污染形势严峻,以可吸入颗粒物(PM10)、细颗粒物(PM2.5)为特征污染物的区域性大气环境问题日益突出,损害人民群众身体健康,影响社会和谐稳定。随着我国工业化、城镇化的深入推进,能源资源消耗持续增加,大气污染防治压力继续加大。为切实改善空气质量,制定本行动计划。

　　总体要求:以邓小平理论、"三个代表"重要思想、科学发展观为指导,以保障人民群众身体健康为出发点,大力推进生态文明建设,坚持政府调控与市场调节相结合、全面推进与重点突破相配合、区域协作与属地管理相协调、总量减排与质量改善相同步,形成政府统领、企业施治、市场驱动、公众参与的大气污染防治新机制,实施分区域、分阶段治理,推动产业结构优化、科技创新能力增强、经济增长质量提高,实现环境效益、经济效益与社会效益多赢,为建设美丽中国而奋斗。

　　奋斗目标:经过五年努力,全国空气质量总体改善,重污染天气较大幅度减少;京津冀、长三角、珠三角等区域空气质量明显好转。力争再用五年或更长时间,逐步消除重污染天气,全国空气质量明显改善。

　　具体指标:到2017年,全国地级及以上城市可吸入颗粒物浓度比2012年下降10%以上,优良天数逐年提高;京津冀、长三角、珠三角等区域细颗粒物浓度分别下降25%、20%、15%左右,其中北京市细颗粒物年均浓度控制在60微克/立方米左右。

(600 字)

 注解

1. 本篇节选自中国国务院在2013年9月出台的《大气污染防治行动计划》,涉及燃煤、工业、机动车、重污染预警等十条措施,被称为"空气国十条"。
2. 《行动计划》在深入研究、反复论证的基础上发布实施。行文符合公文规范,措辞准确严谨,并体现了官方文件的中国特色和文化背景。

Word Bank

中文	English	中文	English
中国梦	China Dream	可吸入颗粒物	PM10
三个代表	Three Represents	细颗粒物	PM2.5
科学发展观	Scientific Outlook on Development		
大气环境	atmospheric environment		
生态文明建设	the construction of ecological civilization		
大气污染防治	air pollution prevention		
小康社会	moderately prosperous society	浓度	concentration

Unit 7

Directions: Please summarize the passage in English. Your summary should be about 150—200 words.

_____
_____
_____
_____
_____
_____
_____
_____
_____
_____

Passage B

London Air Quality Strategy 2011—2015

Poor air quality harms human health and can increase the incidence of cardiovascular and lung disease. The Greater London Authority published a report in 2010, which detailed that an estimated 4,267 premature deaths in London in 2008 could be attributed to long term exposure to fine particles (PM2.5). The City of London has some of the worst air quality in the country. This is primarily due to the density of development and its geographical location.

All local authorities in the United Kingdom are required to assess air quality and identify areas where it is unlikely to meet objectives set by the Government. The objectives have been set at levels at which minimal effects on human health are likely to occur. Air quality in the City does not meet the objectives for both annual average and hourly average nitrogen dioxide, and daily average particulate matter (PM10). As a consequence, the City has been declared an Air Quality Management Area for these two pollutants.

This document sets the strategic direction for air quality policy at the City of London from 2011 until 2015. It outlines steps that the City of London will take, and is already taking, to improve air quality in the City. Some action is already underway such as reducing emissions from the corporate fleet and buildings, and controlling emissions from construction sites and new developments. Other policies and programmes will be developed and implemented over the next few years.

The key aims of the strategy are:

- To reduce the impact of poor air quality on the health of City residents, workers and visitors, particularly those most vulnerable
- To fulfil statutory obligations for local air quality management and assist the UK Government and Mayor of London in meeting air quality Limit Values
- To encourage and implement cost effective measures to reduce emissions of air pollutants in the Square Mile
- To build public awareness and understanding of air quality through the provision of information
- To recognise, reward and disseminate good practice
- To work in partnership with other organisations, to take a lead and help shape national and regional air quality policy.

Dealing with poor air quality in the City requires action from a wide range of organisations. Policy development will, where appropriate, reflect action being taken by the Mayor of London as part of his Air Quality Strategy, "Clearing The Air", and national action, as detailed in the Government's National Air Quality Strategy.

This strategy focuses on action to reduce nitrogen dioxide and course and fine particles (PM10 and PM2.5). The measures outlined, along with those in the Mayor's Air Quality Strategy, will improve air quality in the City. However, the proposed action will not be sufficient to meet the Limit Value for nitrogen dioxide. This requires coordinated national action.

Following publication of this strategy, an annual report will be produced detailing progress with actions, together with the latest monitoring data and any other information that is considered to be relevant in developing air quality policy at the City. For ease of reference, the air quality actions have been listed on the following pages.

The measures that the City of London intend to progress are detailed below. Further information for each action, together with specific outcomes, is included in the body of the document.

- The City of London will continue to monitor air pollutants to ensure that air quality objectives and Limit Values are being met, and to assess the effectiveness of national, regional and local policies to reduce levels of pollution.
- The City of London will ensure that, if possible, policies introduced to improve air quality will also have a positive benefit on reducing greenhouse gas emissions, and policies introduced to reduce greenhouse gas emissions will have a positive benefit on air quality.
- Options for managing traffic in the City to improve air quality locally will be considered during 2011. Air quality impact assessments will be undertaken for transport schemes that involve significant changes to traffic type and movement on City roads.
- The City of London will model the air quality impact of further controls over taxi emissions, the use of low emission buses on routes through the City and a central and inner London Low Emission Zone.
- The City of London will investigate further options for using parking policy to promote the use of low emission vehicles in the Square Mile.
- The City of London will continue to manage its vehicle fleet to reduce emissions of NOx, PM10 and CO_2 year on year.
- The City of London will continue to trial alternatively fuelled vehicles and increase the number of low emission vehicles in the fleet, where appropriate.
- The City will continue to encourage its contractors to use low emission vehicles.
- The City of London will work with public and private bodies to develop low emission procurement guidance.
- The City of London will engage with the City Police to reduce emissions from their fleet.
- The City of London will continue with its efforts to establish effective ways to prevent drivers from leaving vehicle engines idling unnecessarily in the City.
- The City of London will work with the Mayor of London to designate the whole of London no-idling zone.
- The City of London will work with Transport for London to trial a method of dust suppressi

along the route from Victoria Embankment through to Tower Hill.

- If dust suppression is shown to be effective at reducing PM10 concentrations, the City will consider rolling it out to other areas of concern in the Square Mile and encourage Transport for London to apply it on other roads in the City that they are responsible for, particularly Mansell Street and Farringdon Street.

...

1. The passage was excerpted from the official document "City of London Air Quality Strategy 2011—2015," in the website of http://www.cityoflondon.gov.uk/NR/rdonlyres/0115B849-EA52-417D-8ED3-CBCC52B20E1C/0/HS_EH_CityofLondonAirQualityStrategy2011to2015.pdf.
2. As an official document, it has the typical structure and careful and accurate wording, reflecting the western style and culture.

Directions: Please summarize the passage in Chinese. Your summary should be about 200—300 words.

Unit 8

TECHNOLOGY AND MEDIA

What Orwell feared were those who would ban books. What Huxley feared was that there would be no reason to ban a book, for there would be no one who wanted to read one. Orwell feared those who would deprive us of information. Huxley feared those who would give us so much that we would be reduced to passivity and egoism. Orwell feared that the truth would be concealed from us. Huxley feared the truth would be drowned in a sea of irrelevance... In short, Orwell feared that what we hate will ruin us. Huxley feared that what we love will ruin us.

—From Foreword of *Amusing Ourselves to Death*
by Neil Postman

Learning Objectives

Upon completion of this unit, you should be able to:

Remember & Understand	★ recognize and retrieve terms related to media technology; ★ identify and explain in your own words the thesis and the major points of Text A and Text B;
Analyze & Apply	★ use corpora to learn the collocational patterns of a new word; ★ make reference to the thesis and the major points of Text A and Text B in your writing; ★ use sentences or clauses with parallel structure for rhetoric effect;
Evaluate & Create	★ incorporate numbers in descriptive paragraphs; ★ synthesize information about people's attiudes towards media from different sources; ★ deliver a clear and coherent oral presentation of your views on the impact of media on society.

Unit 8

Part One Lead-in

Section 1 Listening

Task 1 Filling in the Blanks

Directions: Please fill in the blanks with one or two words on the basis of what you have heard in the dialogue.

A: What kinds of TV programs do you enjoy watching?

B: I like ___1___ programs and ___2___, especially wildlife ones. How about you?

A: I like those kinds of programs too. They're very ___3___. I think that many people underrate the ___4___ of TV.

B: I agree. People often ___5___ TV for showing too much sex and violence.

A: Yeah. And that's so funny because most people prefer watching sex and violence to watching something more educational!

B: Right. You can't blame the TV stations for showing ___6___ kinds of programs. They need to make money from advertisements shown during and between programs.

A: In my country, there's a ___7___ on the advertisements that can be shown. I think it's about six minutes per hour.

B: That's great idea. But don't the TV stations lose a lot of money because of that?

A: No. they don't. They simply charge higher prices at ___8___. Is there no limit on the amount of advertisements that can be shown on TV in your country?

B: Not as far as I know. We have so many advertisements. The interruptions are ___9___ sometimes! That's one reason that many people prefer satellite or cable TV, where you pay a fixed amount each month.

A: Some people have satellite and cable TV in my country, but people don't seem ___10___ pay for their TV programs. Besides, the terrestrial channels offer a good range of programs.

B: Well, there's a wildlife on TV in a few minutes. Shall we?

Task 2 Group Discussion

Directions: Please discuss the following questions in pairs or groups based on what you have heard.

1. According to the dialogue, what are the positive and negative effects of TV?
2. Can you think of more positive and negative effects of TV?
3. What is your attitude towards TV?

Section 2 Watching

Task 1 Group Discussion

Directions: Please watch the video "Look up" and discuss the following questions in pairs or groups.

1. What was the purpose of the speaker?
2. Why did the speaker make such a proposal?
3. Do you agree with the speaker? Why or why not?

Task 2 Reciting

Directions: Please watch the video again, and try to imitate the speaker to recite the following two stanza in a poetic manner.

All this technology we have, it's just an illusion. Community companionship, a sense of inclusion. Yet when you step away from this device of delusion, you're waken to see a world of confusion.

A world where we're slaves to the technology we mastered, where information gets sold by some rich greedy bastard; a world of self-interest, self-image, self-promotion, where we all share our best bits but leave out the emotion.

Part Two Reading and Writing

Text A

Amusing Ourselves to Death
Neil Postman

1   American television programs are *in demand* all over the world. The total estimate of U.S. television program exports is *approximately* 100,000 to 200,000 hours, equally divided among Latin America, Asia and Europe. Over the years, programs like "Gunsmoke," "Bonanza," "Mission: Impossible," "Star Trek," "Kojak" and more recently, "Dallas" and "Dynasty" have been as popular in England, Japan, Israel and Norway as in Omaha, Nebraska. All of this has occurred *simultaneously* with the decline of America's moral and political *prestige*, worldwide. American television programs are in demand not because America is loved but because American television is loved.

2   We need not be *detained* too long in figuring out why. In watching American television, one is reminded of George Bernard Shaw's remark on his first seeing the *glittering neon signs* of Broadway and 42nd Street at night. It must be beautiful, he said, if you cannot read. American television is, indeed, a beautiful spectacle, a visual delight, pouring forth thousands of images on any given day. The average length of a shot on network television is only 3.5 seconds, so that the eye never rests, always has something new to see. Moreover, television offers viewers a variety of subject matter, requires minimal skills to comprehend it, and is largely aimed at emotional gratification(愉悦). Even *commercials*, which some regard as an *annoyance*, are *exquisitely* produced, always pleasing to the eye and accompanied by exciting music. There is no question but that the best photography in the world is presently seen on television commercials. American television, in other words, is devoted entirely to supplying its audience with entertainment.

Of course, to say that television is entertaining is merely banal (陈腐). Such a fact is hardly threatening to a culture. It may even be a reason for *rejoicing*. Life, as we like to say, is not a highway strewn (撒满) with flowers. The sight of a few *blossoms* here and there may make our journey *a trifle* more *endurable*. But what I am claiming here is not that television is entertaining but that it has made entertainment itself the natural format for the *representation* of all experience. Our television set keeps us *in constant communion with* the world, but it does so with a face whose smiling countenance (面容) is unchangeable. The problem is not that television presents us with entertaining subject matter but that all subject matter is presented as entertaining, which is another issue altogether.

To say it still another way: Entertainment is the supraideology (超意识形态) on television. No matter what is depicted or from what point of view, the primary *presumption* is that it is there for our amusement and pleasure. That is why even on news shows which provide us daily with fragments of tragedy and barbarism (野蛮行为), we are urged by the *newscasters* to "join them tomorrow." What for? One would think that several minutes of murder and mayhem (骚乱) would suffice as material for a month of sleepless nights. We accept the newscasters' invitation because we know that the "news" is not to be taken seriously, that it is all in fun, *so to say*. Everything about a news show tells us this — the good looks and *amiability* of the cast, their pleasant banter (打趣), the exciting music that opens and closes the show, the vivid film *footage*, the attractive commercials — all these and more suggest that what we have just seen is no cause for weeping. A news show, to put it plainly, is a format for entertainment, not for education, *reflection* or catharsis (精神净化). And we must not judge too harshly those who have *framed* it in this way. They are not *assembling* the news to be read, or broadcasting it to be heard. They are televising the news to be seen. They must follow where their medium leads. There is no *conspiracy* here, no lack of intelligence, only a straightforward recognition that "good television" has little to do with what is "good" about *exposition* or other forms of verbal communication but everything to do with what the pictorial images look like.

Film, records and radio are, of course, equally devoted to entertaining the culture, and their effects in altering the style of American discourse are not insignificant. But television is different because it *encompasses* all. No one goes to a movie to find out about government policy or the latest scientific advances. No one buys a record to find out the baseball scores or the weather or the latest murder. No one turns on radio anymore for soap operas or a presidential address. But everyone goes to television for all these things and more, which is why television resonates (引起共鸣) so powerfully throughout the culture. Television is our culture's principal mode of knowing about itself. Therefore — and this is the critical point — how television stages the world becomes the model for how the world is properly to be staged. It is not merely that on the television screen all the world is a stage. It is that off the screen the same idea *prevails*. As *typography* once *dictated* the style of conducting politics, religion, business, education, law and other important social matters, television now takes command. In courtrooms, classrooms, operating rooms, board rooms, churches and even airplanes, Americans no longer talk to each other, they entertain each other. They do not exchange ideas; they exchange images. They do not argue with *propositions*; they argue with good looks, *celebrities* and commercials.

(894 words)

New Words

approximately	[ə'prɒksɪmətli]	*ad.*	close to a particular number or time although not exactly that number or time 大约, 大概
simultaneously	[sɪməl'teɪnɪəsli]	*ad.*	at the same time 同时, 一齐
prestige	[pres'tiːʒ]	*n.*	respect and admiration given to sb. or sth., usually because of a reputation for high quality, success or social influence 威信, 威望
detain	[dɪ'teɪn]	*v.*	to delay sb. for a short length of time 耽搁, 阻住
glitter	['glɪtər]	*v.*	to produce a lot of small bright flashes of reflected light 闪烁, 闪耀
commercial	[kə'mɜːʃəl]	*n.*	an advertisement which is broadcast on television or radio 广告, 广告片
annoyance	[ə'nɔɪəns]	*n.*	sth. that makes you annoyed 令人烦恼、不快的事
exquisitely	[ɪk'skwɪzɪtli]	*ad.*	in a beautify, delicate manner 精致地, 精巧地
rejoice	[rɪ'dʒɔɪs]	*v.*	to feel or show great happiness about sth. 高兴, 欢庆
blossom	['blɒsəm]	*n.*	a small flower, or the small flowers on a tree or plant 花, 群花
endurable	[ɪn'djʊərəbl]	*a.*	capable of being borne though unpleasant 可忍受的, 可忍耐的
representation	[ˌreprɪzen'teɪʃən]	*n.*	a sign, picture, model, etc. of sth. 表现, 表征
constant	['kɒnstənt]	*a.*	that happens all the time or is always there 持续不断的, 重复的
presumption	[prɪ'zʌmpʃən]	*n.*	when you believe that sth. is true without having any proof 假设, 推测
newscaster	['njuːzˌkɑːstər]	*n.*	sb. who reads out the reports on a television or radio news program 新闻播音员; 新闻评论人
amiability	[ˌeɪmɪə'bɪləti]	*n.*	the quality of being friendly and pleasant 亲切, 友善
footage	['fʊtɪdʒ]	*n.*	(a piece of) film esp. one showing an event 电影或电视的连续镜头, 进尺
reflection	[rɪ'flekʃən]	*n.*	serious and careful thought 思考; 反思

Unit 8

frame	[freɪm]	v.	to create and develop 设计；定位
assemble	[əˈsembl]	v.	to come together in a single place or bring parts together in a single group 集合，聚集
conspiracy	[kənˈspɪrəsi]	n.	when people secretly plan together to do sth. bad or illegal 阴谋，密谋
exposition	[ˌekspəˈzɪʃən]	n.	a clear and full explanation of an idea or theory 清楚、详尽的解释；详细阐述
encompass	[ɪnˈkʌmpəs]	v.	to include, esp. different types of things 包含，包括（尤指很多不同事物）
prevail	[prɪˈveɪl]	v.	to be common among a group of people or area at a particular time 流行，盛行
typography	[taɪˈpɑːgrəfi]	n.	the art or practice of printing 印刷；印刷术
dictate	[dɪkˈteɪt]	v.	to give orders, or state sth. exactly, with total authority 决定，规定
proposition	[ˌprɒpəˈzɪʃən]	n.	an idea or opinion 主张；命题
celebrity	[sɪˈlebrɪti]	n.	sb. who is famous, esp. in the entertainment business （尤指娱乐行业）名流，明星

Phrases & Expressions

in demand	greatly desired 所需要的，有需求的
neon sign	glass tubes filled with a colorless gas which shines red when an electric current goes through it 霓虹灯，氖气灯
trifle	slightly 稍微，略微
in communication with	connected with 联系的；有交流的
so to say	if I may say so 可以这么说；因此说

Notes

1. The text was adapted from "The Age of the Show Business," Chapter Six of the book *Amusing Ourselves to Death: Public Discourse in the Age of Show Business*. The book is regarded as one of the most important texts in media study and has been translated into eight languages. In the book, the author Neil Postman argues that the shift in the dominating medium of the American society, i.e. that from typography to television, has changed the way in which people talk, feel and think about fundamental issues in the world.

2. The author of the book, Professor Neil Postman (March 8, 1931—October 5, 2003), was an American author, educator, media theorist and cultural critic. He wrote 18 books and more than 200 magazine and newspaper articles. *Amusing Ourselves to Death*, published in 1985,

is his best-known work. His other major works include *The Disappearance of Childhood* (1982), *Technopoly: the Surrender of Culture to Technology* (1992), and *The End of Education: Redefining the Value of School* (1996).

Task 1   Generating the Outline

Directions: Please identify the thesis of the passage and the main point of each paragraph and find out how these points develop the thesis. You may use the table below to help you.

The thesis:	The huge popularity of American TV programs, which are intended only for entertainment, has made _____.
Para. 1: *The phenomenon:*	American TV programs are _____ all over the world.
Para. 2: *The reason:*	American TV programs are devoted entirely to _____.
Para. 3: *The problem:*	American TV programs have made entertainment _____.
Para. 4: *An example:*	The news show on TV is actually _____.
Para. 5: *The effect:*	The idea that _____ prevails both on and off the screen.

Task 2   Understanding the Text

Directions: Please answer the following questions based on Text A.

1. What is your understanding of the title "Amusing Ourselves to Death"?
2. What was the author's attitude towards television, positive, neutral, or negative?
3. What does "this" refer to in the sentence "All of this has occurred ... worldwide"? (Para. 1)
4. Why is American TV loved all over the world according to the author? (Para. 2)
5. Why did the author cite the remark of Bernard Shaw? (Para. 2)
6. What did the author mean when he wrote that "...it [television] does so with a face whose smiling countenance is unchangeable"? (Para. 3)
7. What did the author mean when he said "Entertainment is the supraideology on television"? (Para. 4)
8. On what basis did the author assert that the news show was actually for entertainment? (Para. 4)
9. According to the author, why did television resonate so powerfully throughout the culture? (Para. 5)
10. Could you explain "they do not argue with propositions; they argue with good looks, celebrities and commercials"? (Para. 5)

Task 3   Vocabulary Building

Directions: Compare and contrast the five most frequent collocational patterns of the following words in different corpora or different parts of the same corpus. Then discuss the implications of the results.

constant   prestige   prevail   presumption   rejoice

constant + n.

word(%)	effort	practice	development	pressure	competition
sino	10.13	4.63	4.63	4.63	4.63
bnc	0.40	0.34	0.17	1.79	0

word(%)	rate	pressure	stream	companion	supply
bnc	2.06	1.79	1.48	1.45	1.32
sino	0	3.99	0	0.75	0

(注:"sino"为句酷批改网作文集,"bnc"为英国国家语料库。数据来源为句酷批改网语料库词典 http://www.pigai.org/corpus/index.php)

Task 4 Learning the Phrases

Directions: Please fill in the blanks in the sentences below with the phrases listed in the box. Change the forms if necessary. Notice that some phrases need to be used more than once.

> v. sb. to death   remind sb. of sth.   in demand
> (be) devoted to   in communication with   so to say

1. I'll be _____ my lawyer about this matter.
2. So, as my whiskers grew, I settled down to watch France beat Brazil in an exciting football match, and enjoy one channel entirely _____ children, where understanding was universal despite the language.
3. It was just that people saying things like that _____ one of my all-time favorite cartoons where Dr. Watson is saying to Sherlock Holmes: "But if you saw the conditions these Moriartys had to live in, you wouldn't be so quick to judge."
4. You frightened me _____, staying out all night!
5. Estate cars capable of carrying seven or even eight people are always _____ —especially Volvos.
6. Her death _____ the dangers of complacency in Africa.
7. The tower provided shore accommodation for keepers and kept _____ the lighthouse by means of flagstaff signals and carrier pigeons.
8. They were unwanted now, unusable, _____, and so they were dying of sheer loneliness.
9. He seems hell-bent on drinking himself _____.
10. The Institute of Export is the only professional body solely _____ enhancing the United Kingdom's export performance.

Task 5 Studying the Sentence Structure

Parallel Clauses and Sentences

Sentences from the text

1. No one goes to a movie to find out about government policy or the latest scientific advances. No one buys a record to find out the baseball scores or the weather or the latest murder. No one turns on radio anymore for soap operas or a presidential address. (Para. 5)
2. They do not exchange ideas; they exchange images. They do not argue with propositions; they argue with good looks, celebrities and commercials. (Para. 5)

Directions: Please follow the example and create two sets of parallel clauses and sentences on your own.

Tips

> 1. Parallel clauses or sentences add power to your writing.
> 2. When creating parallel clauses or sentences, you need to ensure the format of the first clause or sentence be maintained in the subsequent clause(s) or sentence(s).
> 3. You can use conjunctions or semicolons to connect parallel clauses.

1. _____
_____
_____

2. _____
_____
_____

Task 6 Paraphrasing Difficult Sentences

1. American television is, indeed, a beautiful spectacle, a visual delight, pouring forth thousands of images on any given day.
_____
_____

2. Moreover, television offers viewers a variety of subject matter, requires minimal skills to comprehend it, and is largely aimed at emotional gratification.
_____
_____

3. The problem is not that television presents us with entertaining subject matter but that all subject matter is presented as entertaining, which is another issue altogether.
_____
_____

4. One would think that several minutes of murder and mayhem would suffice as material for a month of sleepless nights.
_____
_____

5. They do not argue with propositions; they argue with good looks, celebrities, and commercials.

Task 7   Summarizing the Text

Directions: Please summarize Text A in 100 words. You may use the table in Task 1 to help you.

Task 8   Writing with Numbers

Directions: Write a passage of two paragraphs to support or refute Neil Postman's view through a detailed analysis of a TV program. In the first paragraph, you should summarize Neil Postman's view and state your opinion. In the second paragraph, you should describe and analyze a TV program to support your point. Your writing should be about 200 words. You may use what is provided in the box below to help you.

Tips

1. Hard facts with numbers are often more effective and authoritative than general statements. For instance, in Text A, Neil Postman did not say: "A lot of U.S. television programs are exported." Instead, he spelled it out for you: "The total estimate of U.S. television program exports is approximately 100,000 to 200,000 hours." (Para. 1) Similarly, instead of saying "The average length of a shot on network television is very short," he wrote "The average length of a shot on network television is only 3.5 seconds." (Para. 2)
2. When introducing the TV program, therefore, you may include specific numbers, such as the number of the audience it has, the audience rating of the program, or the hours you (and other people) spend on this program, etc. to make your writing more effective and authoritative.

> Neil Postman, an American author, educator, media theorist and cultural critic, once expressed his deep concerns about television. According to him, [...]. Neil Postman's argument is well-justified/biased.
>
> [...] can be a ready example to support/refute his view. This program [...]

Part Three Reading and Speaking

Text B

Always On: Personal and Cognitive Consequences
Naomi S. Baron

1   You sent your mom flowers for Mother's Day and want to be sure they have arrived. Because they are a surprise, you don't want to call her and ask. The solution? Track the delivery online.

The same *digital* technology that enables us to track packages also makes it possible to track each other. Unless we turn them off, our mobile phones ring when we are meeting with professors, apologizing to girlfriends, or sitting down for dinner at a four-star restaurant.

2   Going the next step, there are mobile phone services that let you know if someone on your mobile network is physically in the *vicinity*. Say you're at a Nationals baseball game in Washington. A helpful message *pops up* on your phone that your friend Matt is also in the stadium. But the same kinds of services *inform* a fourteen-year-old's mother that she's not at school working on a project, as she reported, but actually at the *mall*.

3   Technology has always been Janus-faced. Automobiles are convenient personal modes of transportation, but they *consume* vast quantities of fossil fuels and kill more than 43,000 people a year in the United States alone. Refrigerator *eliminated* the need to go to the market each day but also meant that the food we eat is now less fresh. Modern language technologies *enable* a farmer standing in the fields outside a tiny Spanish town to call San Francisco so his homesick daughter can listen to the local goats being led home for the night, but the same tools have led us into a situation where we are increasingly available as communication targets and we constantly *strategize* how to control social contact. Being "always on" in a networked and mobile world has *consequences*. The costs can be measured in *personal* and *cognitive* terms.

4   How does our *relentless* access to others—and them to us—affect us personally? One obvious result: It leaves many of us exhausted. Another is that this constant contact oftentimes makes us *inefficient*. Genevieve Bell, a small business owner in India, says: my mobile phone makes me mobile, but less efficient. When we had just one phone, and no phone in the factory, and none in the office at all, I felt more efficient... [Now,] if I forget something, I can just call... I spend more money, I am always available, I get nothing done.

5   A more subtle impact of nonstop communication is that it can, *paradoxically*

contribute to a sense of loneliness. Many young people fill the times they are alone (walking across campus, waiting in an airport) by calling or texting friends. The goal is not to share information or even say hello but to avoid being by themselves.

Half a century ago, the *sociologist* David Riesman noted a change occurring in the character of Americans. Where earlier they had been "inner directed" (reflecting their adherence to the norms of adult authority), now those members of the middle and upper-middle class who populated urban areas were increasingly what he called "other directed" (meaning that their behavior was more commonly shaped by their *peer group*). The result, said Riesman, was that the middle-class American "remains a lonely member of the crowd because he never comes really close to the others or to himself."

Riesman's *notion* of the lonely crowd, of people surrounded by others yet nonetheless isolated, has reverberated (回响) over the decades. In earlier days, talk radio has served as an *antidote* for loneliness in urban and rural landscapes alike. Now in the age of blogs and social networking sites, we *savor* reading or viewing highly personal profiles.

Moving to the cognitive *domain*, it seems likely that multitasking will be the 800-pound gorilla challenging users of language and communication technologies. We *multitask* of our own *volition*—or because we are asked to. A study by the New York Families and Work Institute reported that 45 percent of workers in the United States felt they were expected to perform too many tasks at the same time. Are there consequences?

Studies on the cognitive effects of multitasking continue to appear, and the news is sobering. *The bottom line* is that at least for many cognitive tasks, we simply cannot concentrate on two things at once and expect to perform each as well as if we did the tasks individually.

Now a group of neuroscientists (神经学家) has the pictures to prove it. A research team at the Vanderbilt Center for *Integrative* and Cognitive Neurosciences recently published a study in *Neuron*, in which they used an MRI (核磁共振) scanner to record brain activity of subjects performing mental tasks under two different conditions. In both instances, subjects were asked to press a computer key corresponding to one of eight sounds they heard and to speak a vowel corresponding to one of eight graphic images. Under the first condition, the tasks were presented essentially simultaneously, while in the second, they were presented one at a time. Performance on the second task was slower when the two tasks were presented simultaneously than when presented individually. The authors conclude that "a *neural* network of frontal lobe areas (额叶区) acts as a central *bottleneck* of information processing that severely limits our ability to multitask."

John Ratey, a professor of psychiatry (精神病学) at Harvard, has begun speaking of "*acquired deficit disorder*" to describe "the condition of people who are accustomed to a constant stream of digital *stimulation* and feel bored in the absence of it." Ratey is not arguing that information communication technologies such as mobile phones are evil, but rather that they should be used *in moderation*. Drawing an *analogy* between food addiction and addiction to communication devices, Ratey notes that "food is essential for life, but problematic *in excessive doses*. And that's what makes breaking technology addiction so difficult."

(957 words)

Notes

1. This passage was adapted from pages 213—219 of Chapter Ten "The People We Become: The Cost of Being Always On" of the book *Always On: Language in An Online and Mobile World*. The book was written by Naomi S. Baron and published by Oxford University Press in 2008. It won the English-Speaking Union's "The HRH The Duke of Edinburgh English Language Book Award" for 2008.
2. The author of the book Naomi S. Baron is a linguist and professor of linguistics at the Department of Language and Foreign Studies, at American University, in Washington, D.C. Her areas of research include computer-mediated communication, writing and technology, language in social context, language acquisition and the history of English. She is also interested in language use in the computer age, instant messaging, text messaging, mobile phone practices, cross-cultural research on mobile phones, human multitasking behavior, and online social interaction usage by American college students.
3. In ancient Roman religion and myth, Janus is the god of beginnings and transitions, and thereby of gates, doors, doorways, passages and endings. He is usually depicted as having two faces, since he looks to the future and to the past. The derived meaning of "Janus-faced" is having two contrasting aspects.
4. "800-pound gorilla" is an American English expression for a person or organization so powerful that it can act without regard to the rights of others or the law. The phrase is rooted in a joke riddle: "Where does an 800-pound gorilla sit?" The answer: "Anywhere it wants to." This highlights the disparity of power between the "800-pound gorilla" and everything else.

New Words

digital	[ˈdɪdʒɪtl]	a.	(of information, music, an image, etc.) that is... 数码的, 数字的
vicinity	[vɪˈsɪnɪti]	n.	the immediately surrounding area 邻近地区, 附近
inform	[ɪnˈfɔːm]	v.	to tell someone about particular facts 通知, 告知

Unit 8

mall	[mɔl]	n.	a large, usually covered, shopping area where cars are not allowed 商业街，购物中心
consume	[kən'su:m]	v.	to use fuel, energy or time, especially in large amounts (尤指大量地)消耗，花费
eliminate	[ɪ'lɪmɪneɪt]	v.	to remove or take away 排除，消除
enable	[ɪ'neɪbl]	v.	to make someone able to do sth., or to make sth. possible 使能够，使可能
strategize	['strætə‚dʒaɪz]	v.	to make a detailed plan for achieving success in situations such as war, politics, business, industry, or sport 制定战略，制定策略
consequence	['kɒnsɪkwəns]	n.	a result of a particular action or situation, often one which is bad or not convenient (常指不好或不利的)结果，后果
personal	['pɜ:sənl]	a.	relating or belonging to a single or particular person rather than to a group or an organization 个人的，私人的
cognitive	['kɑ:gnətɪv]	a.	connected with thinking or conscious mental processes 感知的；认知的
relentless	[rɪ'lentlɪs]	a.	continuing in a severe or extreme way 持续严厉的，持续强烈的
inefficient	[‚ɪnɪ'fɪʃənt]	a.	not organized, skilled or able to work satisfactorily 低效率的，能力差的
paradoxically	[‚pærə'dɒksɪklɪ]	ad.	in a manner that involves two facts or qualities which seem to contradict each other 自相矛盾地；似是而非地
sociologist	[‚səʊsɪ'ɒlədʒɪst]	n.	someone who studies or is an expert in the study of the relationships between people living in groups, especially in industrial societies 社会学家，社会关系研究者
notion	['nəʊʃn]	n.	(a) belief or idea 观念，看法
antidote	['æntɪdəʊt]	n.	a way of preventing or acting against sth. bad 矫正方法；缓解办法
savor	['seɪvə]	v.	to derive or receive pleasure from, or to take pleasure in 欣赏，享受
domain	[dəʊ'meɪn]	n.	an area of interest or an area over which a person has controlled 领域，领地
multitask	[‚mʌltɪ'tæsk]	v.	to do more than one thing at a time 同时做多件事，同时执行多项任务
volition	[və'lɪʃən]	n.	the power to make your own decisions 决断能力；意志力

integrative	[ˈɪntɪɡreɪtɪv]	a.	tending to combine and coordinate diverse elements into a whole 综合的，一体化的
neural	[ˈnjʊərəl]	a.	involving a nerve or the system of nerves that includes the brain 神经的；神经系统的
bottleneck	[ˈbɒtlnek]	n.	a problem that delays progress 障碍，瓶颈
stimulation	[ˌstɪmjʊˈleɪʃn]	n.	when sth. causes someone or sth. to become more active or enthusiastic, or to develop or operate 刺激，激励
analogy	[əˈnælədʒi]	n.	a comparison between things which have similar features, often used to help explain a principle or idea 类似；类比

Phrases & Expressions

pop up	to appear or happen, especially suddenly or unexpectedly 突然出现；弹出
peer group	the people who are approximately the same age as you and come from a similar social group 同龄群体，同辈群体
the bottom line	the most important fact in a situation 本质内容；最重要的一点
acquired deficit disorder	an illness of the mind or body which is gained rather than inherited 获得性缺陷障碍
in moderation	in a moderate manner or proportion 适中地；适当地
in excessive doses	exceeding the measured amount 过量（使用）

Task 1　Summarizing

Directions: Please find the personal and cognitive costs of being always on in a networked and mobile world mentioned in Text B. Present them in your own words.

Task 2　Synthesizing Information

Directions: The materials we have dealt with in this unit, i.e. the audio clip, the video clip, Text A, and Text B, all express the views of the speakers, the authors, or some other people on a certain type of media. Please work in groups to complete the table below, summarizing the views of these people, grouping the views into pros and cons, and noting down the sources of the views. Two examples are done for you. Please tell the results of your group to the class.

Medium	Pros	
		too much sex and violence(Audio, "People");

Smart phone		

Task 3 Making Comments

Directions: Please give a presentation to comment on WeChat, a popular mobile text and voice messaging communication service in China. You need to first state your view and then provide examples, personal experiences, research results, statistics, quotations, etc. to support your view.

Part Four   Cross Cultural Communication

Passage A

微博"意见领袖"的影响力

谢耘耕　徐颖

目前国内正在形成一种新的舆论形成机制，即微博率先报道，传统媒体不断跟进，通过议题互动，共同掀起舆论高潮……

微博为大众媒介设置议题，往往通过意见领袖得以实现。2011年1月26日，由中国社会科学院农村发展研究所于建嵘教授设立的"随手拍照解救乞讨儿童"微博仅仅开通10余天，粉丝数量达到16万多人，有1000余张网友拍摄的乞讨儿童照片被发布在微博上。截至8日，通过网上照片辨认，已发现被拐卖儿童6个，目前已经被顺利解救。

表1　粉丝数量排名前五的新浪微博用户

排名	用户名	粉丝数	活跃度	影响力	综合排名
1	姚晨	6643108	52484	6	6128
2	微博小秘书	5724190	98939	192	17645
3	小S	5683876	187325	3	71908
4	赵薇	5463064	122172	43	27369
5	蔡康永	5075362	225943	2	108849

……

2010年，中国掀起了一波又一波的"围观"名人微博的热潮，微博的"自媒体"特性使其中的意见领袖受到前所未有的关注。目前，我国报纸发行量过百万（包括100万）的只有19份，而微博粉丝过百万的公众人物远多于此。以新浪微博为例，截至2011年3月8日，粉丝数量超过100万的微博数量为177，公众人物微博占据其中的绝大多数，粉丝数最多的公众人物甚至拥有600多万粉丝，粉丝排名前五的微博如表中所示。关于微博,网上流传着这样一段话:"当你的粉丝超100,你就好像是一本内刊;超1000,你就是个布告栏;超过1万,你就像一本杂志;超过10万,你就是一份都市报;超过100万,你就是一份全国性报纸;超过1000万,你就是电视台。"

(577字)

注解

1. 本篇节选改编自谢耘耕、徐颖的论文《微博的历史、现状与发展趋势》。论文载于《现代传播》2011年第4期(总第177期),第75—80页。
2. 作者谢耘耕系上海交通大学人文艺术研究院教授、博士生导师,新媒体与社会研究中心主任;徐颖系上海交通大学人文艺术研究院博士研究生。

Word Bank

微博	weibo	发布	post
意见领袖	opinion leader	围观	circusee
舆论	public opinion	自媒体	we-media
传统媒体	traditional media	公众人物	public character/figure
议题	topic/issue (for discussion)	粉丝	follower

Directions: Please summarize the passage in English. Your summary should be about 150 — 200 words.

_____
_____
_____
_____
_____
_____
_____

Passage B

Five Types of Social Media Influencers

Raymond Morin

1. What Makes a Good Influencer?

"Influence" is a concept that is difficult to evaluate since it refers to both subjective and objective values, resulting in a measurement of commercial and financial success, reputation and credibility, quality of affiliations and contacts, and charisma and the impact of personality.

For each of these values, the notion of influence may vary from person to person. In fact, in the age of social media, the definition is changing as how to identify influencers. Today, thanks to online applications, all social media users now have the opportunity to stand out and in turn become leaders in respect to their interests. As a result, marketers and public relation professionals are forced to reassess their approach to define the notion influence on social networks.

Influencers on social media are either passionate individuals who turn out to be specialists or professionals involved who use Web 2.0 tools as part of their work. They take advantage of their presence on social networks for personal gain or as representative (or ambassador) of a brand, company or organization. They produce and share relevant content, appealing to the interests of a community. This can result in regularly prompting discussions and interactions that might have influence on behaviors.

2. The Five Types of Social Media Influencers

There are different types of influencers. Klout's matrix of influence offers no fewer than twelve different types of influencers that include: the specialist, the activist, the socializer, the observer to the broadcaster, the curator to the thought leader (see Table 1). Many users do not give great importance to this matrix.

Table 1 Klout's matrix of influence

	sharing		creating		
participating	**Curator** You find the most interesting info & share it widely.	**Broadcaster** You broadcast great content that spreads like wildfire.	**Tastemaker** You know what you like; your audience likes it too!	**Celebrity** You are the height of influence — for better or worse.	broad
	Syndicator You keep tabs on what/who is "HOT" & important to watch.	**Feeder** Your audience relies on you for a steady flow of focused information.	**Thought Leader** People look to you to help them to understand the day's development in the industry.	**Pundit** You don't just share news; you create the news.	
	Dabbler You may be just starting out with the social web, or you are just not that into it.	**Conversationalist** You love to connect & always have the inside scoop.	**Socializer** You are the hub of the social scene & people count on you to find out what's happening.	**Networker** You connect to the right people & share generously your network to help followers.	
listening	**Observer** You don't share much, but you follow the social web more than you let on.	**Explorer** You constantly are trying out new ways to interact & network.	**Activist** You've got an idea or a cause to share with the world.	**Specialist** You may not be a celebrity, but in your area of expertise your opinion is second to none.	focused
	causal		consistent		

Lisa Barone, in contrast, proposes that there are roughly five main types of influencers on social media (see table 2):

Table 2 Barone's five types of social media influencers

The networker (Social Butterfly)	One who has the biggest contact list and is found on all platforms. He or she knows everybody and everybody knows him or her.
The opinion leader (Thought Leader)	One who can become the best ambassador of a brand. He or she has built a strong authority in his or her field based on credibility. Their messages are most often commented on and retweeted.
The discoverer (Trendsetter)	One who distributes information to the bloggers to journalists through the specialized webzines. He or she usually amplify messages.
The sharer (Reporter)	Constantly on the lookout for new trends, they become the "hub" in the sector.
The user (Everyday Customer)	One that represents the regular customer. He or she does not have a network as large as the networker, but his or her network remains equally important.

Which kind of influencer do you identify yourself as?

(681 words)

 Notes

1. The passage was retrieved and adapted from: http://www.socialmediatoday.com/content/five-types-social-media-influencers?_tmc=1JuMwuQt7V2eHSwHeuQ-ZLyDKFAwHV_6HgsREsNFsW8.
2. It was originally written by Raymond Morin who is an author, blogger, social media consultant, and content curator. He published two books (in French): *Comment entreprendre le virage 2.0* (2010), and *Culture Web à la portée des PME* (2001). In early 2013, he published his third book: *Business et médias sociaux—Les clés de la Génération Cet du marketing d'influence*, in French, as in English.

Directions: Please summarize the passage in Chinese. Your summary should be about 200—300 words.